PRAISE FOR
BECOMING WISE

"Not every book you read will challenge you to think differently. This book certainly will. Dr. Lesley Corbin has done a stupendous job with this complex subject, balancing a compelling narrative with expert research. Her account of growing up in a tremendously racist culture is deeply touching and inspiring. It demonstrates her resilience and wisdom even at a young age. This book is unquestionably a great read for people of all walks of life."

—**DILIP V. JESTE**, MD, DIRECTOR OF GLOBAL RESEARCH
NETWORK ON SOCIAL DETERMINANTS OF MENTAL HEALTH
AND EXPOSOMICS, LA JOLLA, CALIFORNIA, PRESIDENT-
ELECT, WORLD FEDERATION FOR PSYCHOTHERAPY, AND
EDITOR-IN-CHIEF, INTERNATIONAL PSYCHOGERIATRICS.

"Lesley Corbin is on to something here. Wisdom is generally regarded as a good thing but what is it and why? Through inspiring stories and a commanding tour across the wide breadth of human experience, Lesley begins to answer those important questions. You would be wise to read this book!"

—**LAURENCE FUMAGALLI**, PARTNER,
SCHRODERS GREENCOAT

"Lesley Corbin has gifted us with a straight-forward, highly readable book, filled with portraits of wise actions that prompt us to reflect on our own."

—**WILLIAM R. TORBERT**, LEADERSHIP PROFESSOR EMERITUS, BOSTON COLLEGE, FOUNDING BOARD, GLOBAL LEADERSHIP ASSOCIATES AND AMARA COLLABORATION

"We all have the potential to become wiser. In Becoming wise: A psychological exploration, Dr. Corbin beautifully guides the reader through a journey to understanding and defining our own authentic sense of wisdom. The knowledge that the reader gains from this book will last a lifetime."

—**VICTORIA SHIROMA WILSON**, ED.D., AUTHOR, EXCEPTIONAL FUTURES: THE POWER OF IDENTITY TO DESIGN POSITIVE CHANGE

"In a world where we need wisdom more than ever, not least in our leaders, and for the sake of future generations, this book offers a stimulating, intelligent and illuminating discussion encouraging us to have more self-awareness. It is written with succinct clarity, focussed in its use of academic sources, but never dull, condescending or overwhelming. Most of all this is an accessible read with fascinating stories that beautifully illustrate what wisdom (and the lack of) can and does mean."

—**CAROLINE BUCHAN**, BARRISTER, MEDIATOR AND COMPANY SECRETARY.

BECOMING WISE

BECOMING WISE

A PSYCHOLOGICAL EXPLORATION

Lesley M. Corbin, Ph.D.

MANUSCRIPTS
PRESS

BECOMING WISE
A Psychological Exploration

ISBN   979-8-88926-730-0   Paperback
         979-8-88926-731-7   Ebook
         979-8-88926-732-4   Hardcover

My beloved, Yeshua.
Your wisdom still takes my breath away!

And

My husband, Graham.

My better half, your beautiful mind continues to raise my game.
May you continue to illuminate us with your wisdom!

CONTENTS

Blessed are those who find wisdom,
those who gain understanding,

for she is more profitable than silver
and yields better returns than gold.

She is more precious than rubies;
nothing you desire can compare with her.

Long life is in her right hand;
in her left hand are riches and honor.

Her ways are pleasant ways,
and all her paths are peace.

She is a tree of life to those who take hold of her;
those who hold her fast will be blessed.

PROVERBS 3:13–18, NIV.

INTRODUCTORY THOUGHTS

South Africa was still under apartheid rule when I was born. I grew up, a girl of color, in a society structured to subjugate and limit me from reaching my potential. I had two choices: follow the rules and be mediocre; or buck the system and follow my dreams. Which would be the wiser? The path I chose would shape the direction of my future and would impact my entire life.

Perhaps, given my background and with the benefit of hindsight, I shouldn't be too surprised that I grew to be intrigued by wisdom; by who and what is wise and, more often, not.

My single mother raised me in my maternal grandparents' tin-shack in Athlone, originally a colored township in Cape Town. Life for people of color was tough. Apartheid deemed non-whites to be sub-human. If you were poor, as we were, it was even tougher. The apartheid system conditioned people of color to lack aspiration. Even my own community told us, "You'll never amount to much, you shouldn't dream big, you can't aspire to that." Our teachers' attitude was, "We didn't achieve, so you're not going to either." However, an unintentional but positive consequence of growing up in a system like this was that I became determined to improve my life and achieve all I thought I was capable of.

The education system for people of color was of a very low standard, so much so that we referred to it as "gutter-education." But, somehow, I knew education was the key to unlock the kind of future I desired. I set my sights on going to the University of Cape Town, a school reserved mainly for whites, and which allowed entry to only a small quota of people of color. In 1986, I started my studies there, majoring in clinical psychology to gain a deep understanding of human behavior.

After completing my first degree, my mother decided it was time that I got a job and contributed toward payment of bills. At the time, I was devastated to not be able to continue my studies, especially as many of my friends were. What seemed to be an unkind decision at the time worked in my favor eventually, because it was through my job I realized I wanted to work in a corporate setting and with people who were motivated to improve.

In 1994, quite by chance, I found out about the Fulbright Scholarship, one of the most widely recognized and prestigious scholarships in the world. I was one of only two applicants that year from South Africa to receive a Principal Scholarship, fully funded and all inclusive. I was accepted at Columbia University in New York City to study for a master's in organizational psychology. In 1995, I traveled to the United States to take up my scholarship, my first trip outside South Africa. When the Fulbright Foundation told me I had been granted the scholarship, I was also told my entire life was about to change. I could never have imagined how true those words would become.

One of the doors my scholarship opened was to secure a highly sought-after intern placement at Professor Warner Burke's consulting firm. He is a world-renowned expert in organizational and leadership development, and his firm worked exclusively with C-suite leaders of many premier companies in the US.

Whilst working at Warner's firm, I saw how much the behavior of the leaders impacted the culture, climate, and behaviors throughout an organization. I realized that leaders must first be good people before they can be good leaders, and if one could change their behavior for the better, any attempted organizational transformations were more likely to succeed. This ignited my interest in, and study of, what constitutes human psychological development at its most advanced level. I decided to pursue a PhD in leadership and started my doctoral work in 2002 at the University of Cambridge.

My PhD explored whether a sample of UK C-suite leaders exhibited abilities and behaviors associated with higher levels of psychological development. My findings were illuminating: Very, very few scored at the top levels, which, perhaps, raises some important questions about the selection and development of senior business leaders. During my studies, I learned that high levels of psychological development are associated with wisdom. Little did I know this discovery would drive my work for years to come and eventually lead to this book.

Now I use what I learned from my doctoral research in my work as an organizational psychologist and executive coach. I use it to try to influence my clients to adopt more of the mindsets and behaviors associated with wise people. When successful, I am still fascinated to see how their lives transform and how that impacts those around them. The change can be so profound that it is not uncommon for spouses and partners to comment. I have come to realize that if more people knew and pursued the advantages associated with higher levels of psychological development and wisdom, it could have extraordinarily positive implications for their relationships, businesses, and society at large.

People considering their own development or improvement tend to be focused on, and driven by, self-centered, materialistic values such as a more prestigious job, a higher salary, a bigger house, a fancier car, or more luxurious holidays. The way we are raised and socialized can direct us to self-promotion, material success, and power, not to be other-focused or to consider the benefit of others. We are not overtly encouraged to have values such as benevolence, humility, and gratitude, all of which cultivate the growth of wisdom.

One of the reasons so few people try to become wise is because they do not know how to. Societal role models are sorely lacking. The path is little known. Whilst the behaviors and benefits associated with wisdom are known to the academics who research and write about it, most of this work is largely unknown to the wider public. Yet the knowledge, if made more accessible, absorbed, and applied, holds colossal potential transformative power. So, I have written this book to try to get the message out in a format that is accessible, less theoretical, and wholly practicable.

As Nic M. Weststrate, assistant professor of educational psychology, University of Illinois Chicago, and Judith Glück, professor of developmental psychology, University of Klagenfurt, Austria, note, "Wisdom is a hallmark of optimal human development—a rare personal resource that benefits both society in a broad sense and the individual who wields it" (2017, 800).

Roman philosopher Seneca believed, "Many people could attain wisdom if they were not convinced that they had already done so."

Whilst most of us might like to be wiser, becoming wise is no easy feat. It requires intense psychological work and self-discovery to attain wisdom, but we can all be wiser. Once attained, there are myriad benefits. These include a much deeper understanding of, and ability to regulate, one's own emotions and a much-enhanced perception and understanding of problem variables and their interrelatedness. These open up multiple perspectives to viewing and solving problems; make more comfortable perceptions of ambiguity, risk, and uncertainty; and lengthen the time-horizon of solutions and consequences considered.

Monika Ardelt, a professor and wisdom researcher at the University of Florida, believes very few people attain the necessary levels of psychological development because the road to becoming wise is long, arduous, and involves many hours of self-reflection. In our interview she said, "If you understand yourself better, you can accept your own faults and weaknesses more. This often leads to greater tolerance toward other people and more compassion for them." The very few wise people Ardelt has found all display extremely high levels of self-knowledge, compassion, and humility. The way they view obstacles, problems, and crises differentiates them markedly from those who are not wise.

Judith Glück has done some ground-breaking work into how people grow in wisdom. When we spoke, she said, "Wise people are fascinated with life. They are deeply interested in understanding, learning, and growing." She refers to them as being on a "growth pathway." What separates them from others is that they tend to reflect on their life experiences by exploring and thinking deeply about them. They ask themselves questions such as, "What is most important to me?" "What should my priorities be?" "What might I want to change about the way I live?" Reflecting on such questions changes and equips them to support others in similar situations.

The way in which we choose to behave impacts not only our fellow humans but the entire planet. Each decision we make has ripple effects much further out than most of us can see or imagine. If we had more wisdom, we would better see the interrelationships among things and circumstances. It would enable us to discern, identify, and frame a problem before it is fully formed, opening a wider path to possible solutions. Instead of focusing solely on our own issues and those in our immediate circle, we might look further afield and, in so doing, help those who are in need of our service. Perhaps this book will challenge you to think more about how you might grow your own capacity to be wiser.

Many believe the world is in disarray. We are grappling with large-scale problems that have monumental impacts globally. These include climate change, population growth, and resource shortages, to name a few. A common thread in each of these phenomena is a lack of wise behavior and wise leadership.

Would it not be better if our leaders—political, business, or other—were selected on the basis of their wisdom rather than from those in pursuit of power and status? Should this not be our expectation, indeed our right, since their decisions affect us, our children, and generations to come? Yet an alarming abundance of unwise leaders whose daily decisions, or lack thereof, demonstrates so clearly why wisdom is needed on a global scale.

However, isn't there equally a responsibility on each of us also to demonstrate wisdom in our daily lives? Whilst we might criticize a lack of wisdom in those in leadership positions, should we not also be prepared to develop our own capacity for wise acts?

"Wisdom is the right use of knowledge. To know is not to be wise. Many men know a great deal and are all the greater fools for it. There is no fool so great as a knowing fool. But to know how to use knowledge is to have wisdom."
—CHARLES H. SPURGEON, PASTOR AND AUTHOR

If you would like to grow in wise thoughts, wise emotions, and wise actions, then this book may be for you. As you read it, I hope you are stimulated to consider wise behavior as something you can try to build into your daily life.

Part one will explore what wisdom is, consider some disasters associated with a failure to apply wisdom, and sketch a brief overview of how our understanding of wisdom has developed from its earliest mention to the latest developments in neuroscience. Part two will discuss the hallmarks of wisdom: wise thoughts, wise emotions, wise morality, and wise reflections. Part three will show some ways to grow in wisdom and showcase a few extraordinary people who demonstrated some form of wisdom.

If you would like to leave a more impactful legacy by making wiser decisions, a legacy that lives on much longer than you, then read on. I'm writing with the hope that, as you turn the pages of this book, you will be inspired to start your own journey to becoming wise.

PART I

WHAT IS WISDOM, AND WHY DOES IT MATTER?

CHAPTER ONE

WHAT IS WISDOM?

"It is awfully sad that with our clever brains, capable of taking us to the moon and developing all these sophisticated ways of communicating around the planet, that we seem to have lost wisdom; and that's the wisdom of indigenous people who would make a major decision based on how that decision would affect people seven generations ahead... So, although we think we're caring about our children and grandchildren, we're actually stealing their future."

—JANE GOODALL, RENOWNED NATURALIST
AND CONSERVATIONIST

The words of Jane Goodall, captured in Andrew Zuckerman's book, *Wisdom* (2008, 83), clearly embodies the behavior we as a species are still exhibiting. Several years after Goodall's sage words, we seem still to behave with too little regard for our future generations and the future of our planet.

Our thinking, she implies, is inconsistent with our behavior. As a species we have come exceedingly far with regards to levels of innovation and our ability to cope with technological advances. However, as the "self-pro-claimed" most intelligent species ever to have lived (on our planet), we may also be the first to knowingly pursue a path toward self-destruction (Sternberg 2017, 52). We have failed to consider the long-range consequences of some of our decisions. Future generations are going to have to deal with the effects of our actions and inac-tions—even more extreme weather, drought, flood, food shortages, mass population migration, and the economic and political instability these things will cause.

Goodall says further, "We're making decisions now based on the bottom line. How will this affect me now? Me and my family, now? How will this huge decision affect the next shareholders' meeting three months ahead? How will this decision I make today affect my election cam-paign?" (Zuckerman 2008, 83).

While Goodall made this observation in the 2000s, Erik Erikson, developmental psychologist and psychoanalyst, voiced similar concerns in 1988. Erikson spoke about our inability to consider future generations in how we live and to consider the long-range consequences of the deci-sions we make daily.

On June 14, 1988, Daniel Goleman, renowned for popu-larizing "emotional intelligence," interviewed Joan and Erik Erikson in their Massachusetts house to talk about Erik Erikson's major contributions to psychology. Erik-son opined:

The only thing that can save us as a species is seeing how we're not thinking about future generations in the way we live. What's lacking is generativity, a generativity that will promote positive values in the lives of the next generation. Unfortunately, we set the example of greed, wanting a bigger and better everything, with no thought of what will make it a better world for our great-grandchildren. That's why we go on depleting the earth: we're not thinking of the next generations (Goleman 1988).

Has our technologically advanced world resulted in us becoming so myopic, lacking foresight and, perhaps, far too focused on "what's in it for me?" We have become a people of immediate gratification, googling what we don't know but not then thinking about and reflecting upon it, Amazon-ing what we want over and above what we need, passing acerbic comments on social media platforms without thought of potential consequence, and so on. Our planet is severely burdened by overpopulation and with that comes immense strain on resources, infrastructure, and environment. Our natural inclination is to crave clarity, certainty, and control, but as our world becomes more interconnected and, concomitantly, more complex, we are increasingly in need of something that can help us navigate the complexity. Could the cultivation of wisdom in each of our lives help us as a species become less materialistic and more aware of consequences?

Homo sapiens translates from the Latin as meaning "wise man," which reflects the greater endowment of brain power compared to our predecessors (Encyclopedia). We highly esteem those whom we regard as wise. Wisdom may very well sit at the apex of human behavior. There isn't a continent on earth where wisdom isn't recognized and revered, yet when asked how many wise people we know, we struggle to answer.

Could this be because of our lack of understanding of what wisdom actually is? We certainly don't all get taught about the benefits of wisdom in schools or universities. Most people, if asked whether they know of at least one wisdom exemplar, will probably think of someone like Nelson Mandela. Yet we may not know what it is these wise people do that makes them wise. Perhaps if we did, we could take steps to incorporate it into our own lives.

WHAT IS WISDOM?

Why does wisdom evoke such feelings of reverence in us?

From the interviews that I've conducted and the individuals with whom I've spoken in the process of researching this book, it is evident that most people have some notion of what wise behavior looks like. They may not have an encyclopedic account to hand, but they are able to describe something of what a wise person says or does to merit the title. In response to the question, "Who is the wisest person you know, and why are they wise?" one interviewee said of the person they named:

> *Some people just go right through life, but she is very circumspect. There's a 360 approach to her thinking, and I think that's what makes her wise. There's a*

thoroughness to her, and that's part of what I mean by 360. She plans, she thinks things through, she anticipates things, considers different angles, navigates things thoroughly and deeply. She's also got a lot of empathy and compassion, and she's no fool, and that's wisdom too.

Another interviewee's answer was:

She's a very gentle, very reflective person, which I think helps me to be more reflective. She'd listen to what I had to say and didn't come back with any instant reactions. She would think about it and reflect on it. When she came back with a response, it was with comments that addressed my needs at the time. Her advice was directed to me as an individual, as in what might help me personally, not anyone else. She would give me solutions I could either take or not, but she was able to identify with my emotions and feelings and had a real empathy for what I was experiencing.

As I listened to these and the other interviewees and thought about their descriptions of a wise person, something about wisdom became apparent to me. They were not describing something or someone mythical, enigmatic, or perfect. They were describing someone who employs thoughtful consideration of others, planning and anticipating what might come next, and demonstrating an empathy and compassion customized toward the needs of the person or persons with whom they are dealing. These are not actions reserved only for wise exemplars. These are actions you and I can strive toward in our daily lives if we so desire.

MY VIEWS OF WISDOM

I think of wisdom, ultimately, as the pinnacle of human development. It is adult psychological development at its most advanced. But I do not view wisdom as an end-state. Rather, I see it as a continuum, a path on which the participants interact and deal with their life challenges, their faults, their fears, then navigating, managing, and embracing them. I, like others, believe one cannot be completely wise, much like one cannot attain a state of complete self-awareness. Everyone who actively seeks, and some who may attain without seeking, is somewhere along the journey.

The sentiments of two authors support this view: Caroline Bassett, founder of The Wisdom Institute, Minneapolis, who said, "Wisdom lies on a continuum... from the extraordinary to the everyday" (2011, 304), and Stephen Hall, journalist and author, who said the "demand for wisdom is thrust upon us on a daily basis in matters momentous and mundane" (2010, 267).

A wise person seeks the common good and balances the interests of multiple parties short-term and long-term when making decisions (Sternberg 1998, 350; Sternberg, Glück, and Karami 2022, 55). Their actions and decisions consider universal values such as benevolence, fairness, honesty, and integrity, and accordingly they behave consistently toward others in the way they think everyone should be treated. The wise person penetrates beyond the surface of a problem to its essentials with unbiased clarity, to identify the salient dimensions and alternatives, to provide advice, guidance, and practical solutions.

A good example of someone who behaved like this, making everyone she spoke to feel valued, was Agnes Morgan-Smith, businesswoman, philanthropist, and pioneer. I first met Agnes in South Africa in 1998. Sadly, she passed away in 2011. I spoke to her daughter, Annemarié, who shared her mother's story with me.

Agnes was born in 1913. She wanted to study law and work for the rights and justice of others, but financial constraints prevented this. Undeterred, Agnes worked her way up in the business world, eventually purchasing a company which supplied electrical and engineering equipment in what was then a highly competitive "man's world."

During the 1950s, Agnes began her involvement in various charitable organizations, giving freely of her time, campaigning especially for the less privileged. While serving as president of the National Council of Women in Port Elizabeth, South Africa, Agnes founded the Consumers Association (their first chapter) and later became the president. The Consumers Association rapidly spread to all major cities in South Africa. Later, she moved to Cape Town, where she became a committee member of the Chamber of Commerce. She remained so well into her eighties.

One of her campaigns for the Consumers Association during the 1950s concerned margarine and South Africa's low-income families. At this time, margarine was white, unappetizing, and looked like lard. Other countries were starting to add a yellow dye, which greatly improved its appearance. Agnes successfully campaigned for South Africa to follow suit despite resistance from the minister of agriculture and the powerful farming lobby, who realized they would lose butter sales to the much cheaper margarine which would be bought by South Africa's very many poor.

In her mid-eighties and still a committee member of the Chamber of Commerce in Cape Town, Agnes noticed bus stops along a busy seaside road, used particularly by many domestic workers and shopping mall shift-workers, gave no shelter from bad weather. She set about liaising with a member of parliament, and within months new covered bus stops were installed. By then, her reputation carried a significant momentum of its own, always an asset in getting things done.

She had the enviable ability to communicate with each person on their own level, from heads of state, politicians, and CEOs to domestic workers. She always gave each person her undivided attention, which made them feel significant. When they asked her for advice, they would feel they'd received valuable, positive guidance.

Agnes achieved a great deal during her lifetime. Her daughter told me, "She was written up in several publications, including Who's Who in the World, the Top 1,000 Women in the World, the Who's Who of Southern Africa, and was the recipient of numerous awards." When Agnes was interviewed for a national newspaper about her many involvements in charitable organizations and accomplishments in commerce and business, she was asked what she considered to be her greatest achievement. Without hesitation, she replied, "It has been the privilege of being of service to my fellow human beings."

When I asked Annemarié to describe her mother in a few words, she didn't rush to point out her intellect or her numerous achievements, but merely stated, "Great fun." Agnes, like many wise people, had a contagious sense of humor. She was a woman of great faith in her God. She faced challenges, as we all do, but tended to live her life with a light touch and an ease. She lived her life with honesty, integrity, and passion.

I remember Agnes well. She had an insatiable curiosity. She was a deep thinker and asked penetrating questions. She was fearless and tenacious. Yet there was a gentleness to her that was very disarming. In chapter five, you will read about a concept termed "enlightened self-interest," where people of moral excellence merge their self-interests with the pursuit of helping others. Agnes personified this. She was always looking for and finding ways to be of service to others. This is one of the essential characteristics I associate with wise people.

Something I have come to observe with wise people is that they have foresight. They see what could happen next, perceiving problems well before they are fully formed. Of the wise people I've had the privilege of knowing, one of the things that sets them apart from those I didn't consider wise is that they appear almost prescient. They have deep discernment to see through problems, situations, and people so they can fully grasp the situation from its multitude of perspectives.

Imagine you're faced with an extremely complex and thorny situation, with many dimensions and solutions. You don't know what to do. You would like someone's advice. Think of who in your life you would choose to ask for advice, and then think, *Why that person?*

I'm at a huge advantage, because the person I would choose is my husband, Graham. Everyone who knows him will agree he is highly intelligent, and the solutions he proposes are sometimes unusual, creative, and undoubtedly novel. He once managed to get someone out of a binding contract by coming up with a most creative solution, which a very highly esteemed employment/contract lawyer had failed to identify. Graham is not a lawyer, nor has he had any legal training. It's not because of his impressive intellect he comes up with novel solutions. It's as though he has knowledge of something he could not possibly have, and this somehow informs his thoughts and actions. We've been married for more than twenty years, and I have witnessed this behavior time and again.

Coupled with this apparent prescience is the capacity to see a vast array of perspectives. He cleverly balances the emotions concerning the situation and what the other person or persons might be experiencing, and he thinks about how the issues could play out in a multitude of ways. He then presents the person with options, from least to most likely acceptable to them. He suggests (only if asked) solutions that take account of their personality. What I always find amusing are the questions he asks. It's as though they've come out of left field; you don't see them coming.

I noticed this with Agnes Morgan-Smith too. She also seemed to ask questions that divert one's attention to why it's being asked, rather than focusing on what the answer might be. If you're analytical, you'll try to work out why it's being asked. However, when Graham asks a further question, you realize you haven't got a clue where he's going with his line of questioning. Yet, somehow, at some point during his questions, you realize you now see the problem from a different perspective or with new insight, and solutions seem clearer and simpler. This stems from his ability to make connections where others have perhaps failed to see them. Whilst he has no difficulty regulating his own emotions, his focus will be on others to try to help them regulate theirs whilst presenting the various consequences of taking a particular solution path.

One of the things I particularly enjoy about Graham is his ever-curious nature. Many times, he is like a little boy fascinated by things: never childish, but childlike. I think of wise people as being fascinated by life, increasingly curious about how it all works, an uncanny ability to not take themselves too seriously, and a great sense of humor.

I have also seen this childlike fascination, coupled with a boundless sense of humor, in one of my mentors, Eileen, whom I consider to be wise. She embodies the very essence of curiosity, love for and of learning, and humility that has been written about by many wisdom researchers. But what really makes me think she's wise is her ability to access a broad range of emotional responses, and she can see the range from multiple perspectives. If you don't know her, she might come across as quite measured emotionally, but I have come to see this as her management of emotion, suspending of judgment until all the facts have been aired, and then, much like I have seen with Graham, she presents the possible solutions to consider. Her incredible sense of humor brings a certain ease to the situation.

I don't know many wise people, but I know a few, and I would say it is the way they live or have lived their lives, and how they dealt with their life challenges, that identifies them as wise. This does not mean they do or will not have moments of being unwise, nor that their lives are in any way perfect. Rather, their lives reveal humility, gratitude for what they have, compassion toward self and others, and concern for issues beyond self. They seem each to have a robust moral compass.

"Wisdom is not simply an accumulation of knowledge: it is a way of being and doing"
(ROONEY, MCKENNA, LIESCH, AND BOAL 2008, 344).

WHAT WISDOM IS NOT

When I spoke to Bill Torbert, leadership professor emeritus at Boston College, Massachusetts, he was emphatic about what wisdom is not. "One of the mistakes in our culture is to confuse expertise for wisdom," he said. He further explained that expertise can be seen as conditional confidence within specific domains, "like an operating room or a law court, and you're very good at what you do there."

WISDOM AND EXPERTISE

Wise people, he said, approach issues and subjects with a certain confidence, even if they don't know anything about them, which he termed "unconditional confidence." This, he explained, "is where you are confident even if you don't know anything about the situation. So, while you approach it with humility, you also approach it with the kind of confidence that you're not going to be reduced to helplessness because you don't know anything specific about the situation." He said, "Instead the wise become more attentive and listen more deeply so that they may learn."

I agree with Torbert that expertise can be mistaken for wisdom, and I have witnessed this in my dealings with "subject matter" experts. They have a confidence about their knowledge, which exudes an attitude of, "I'm well acquainted with this subject." This can mistakenly lead others to see them as wise because they have insights others may not, but years of accumulated knowledge is not the same as wisdom. Although wise people have a certain expertise when it comes to dealing with ambiguity, complexity, and uncertainty, wisdom is so much more than expertise.

We know that expertise and wisdom are not the same, even though people may confuse the two. However, two other concepts are even more commonly mistaken for wisdom: intelligence and creativity. Let's have a look at how these concepts overlap but are distinct from wisdom.

WISDOM AND INTELLIGENCE

Wisdom researchers agree that intelligence is not sufficient to make a person wise and that wisdom is a more
multidimensional and multifaceted concept than intelligence (Ardelt 2005, 8; Glück and Scherpf 2022, 649).

Pioneering wisdom researcher and geriatric neuropsychologist, Vivian Clayton, sees wisdom as "the ability to
grasp human nature, which is paradoxical, contradictory,
and subject to continual change." She sees intelligence
as "the ability to think logically, to conceptualize and
abstract from reality" (Clayton 1982, 316). Furthermore,
Clayton sees wisdom as "provoking the individual to consider the consequences of his actions both to self and
their effects on others. Wisdom, therefore, evokes questions of should one pursue a particular course of action"
(Clayton 1982, 315).

Intelligence is defined by Sternberg as "the ability to
learn, reason, and adapt to the environment" (2022, 5).
It is a measure of how well individuals adapt to their
surroundings (Sternberg 2019, 3-4). People have varying
degrees of adaptation, but usually these are in pursuit
of self-benefit and at the expense of others. Wise people
pursue things to benefit others, not at their expense nor
for personal gain.

I see three significant ways in which intelligence differs
from wisdom. The first concerns Sternberg's definition
of intelligence (one's ability to adapt skillfully to one's
environment) and Clayton's characterization of wisdom
(consideration of consequences of one's actions on self

and on others). This differentiates between intelligence and wisdom. You may recall the intelligent seek to make decisions that benefit themselves and their immediate circle, not the common good. The wise, however, do consider the common good and how the short- and the long-range consequences of decisions they take might impact others.

The second is humility. Wise people understand the limits of their knowledge. They do not know everything and do not have all the answers. Furthermore, they have no difficulty acknowledging this. They display humility. This is not so for all intelligent people. Intelligence can entail a tendency to believe that one has all the answers. This is intellectual arrogance and vanity, and it displays a certain fragility. Is this perhaps why Socrates (discussed in the next chapter) and other philosophers were so keen to promote the conception of wisdom as knowing what you do not know or accepting the limitations of your own knowledge? Were they seeking to demonstrate the difference between "intellectual arrogance" and "intellectual humility"?

The third concerns morality or ethical behavior. Sternberg noted, "Intelligence without wisdom is not enough and, indeed, can be a dangerous thing" (1986, 177). Intelligence can be deployed to good ends. Chapter three will illustrate how one woman's consideration of the long-range consequences of her decisions mitigated a cataclysmic disaster. But intelligence can also be used for evil. Two such examples are Hitler and Stalin.

In chapter five, I point out that we prioritize those things to which we attach value and that our behavior flows from what we value. The value orientations of wise individuals are focused on a greater good to balance the interests of all parties concerned, and these may perhaps extend as far out as Goodall suggests at the outset of this chapter—"seven generations ahead." Because the wise consider many perspectives when thinking about moral issues and dealing with the emotional and social aspects of complex situations, they will act ethically in testing situations whilst the intelligent may not.

Experts tell us that intelligence is a necessary but not sufficient condition for wisdom (Glück and Scherpf 2022, 649). But what of creativity—is it also necessary for wisdom?

WISDOM AND CREATIVITY

Creativity is not synonymous with wisdom. Creative people are not necessarily wise, but it is more than likely that wise people possess levels of creativity that contribute to their ability to generate novel and unusual solutions to ill-defined or wicked problems. Wicked problems are complex, often intractable. They have no clear-cut solution, any apparent solution often generates other problems, and there is no right or wrong answer, but there are better or worse alternatives (Grint 2005, 1473; Kitchener and Brenner 1990). These characteristics are quite typical of problems that require wisdom (Judith Glück personal correspondence April 2023).

Dean Keith Simonton, distinguished professor of psychology at the University of California, Davis, is a pioneer in the field of the psychological study of creativity. In his view, to qualify as creative, something needs to be original, adaptive or practical, and influential (2002, 191). Creativity can be an idea, process, or product. Simonton believes creativity is among the most important of all human activities. Such is the importance of creativity to society that a legal framework has been developed to protect it, which includes patent, copyright, and intellectual property laws. And the creative industry honors its best performers with, for example, Academy Awards (Simonton 2002, 189).

Francesca Gino, professor at Harvard, and Dan Ariely, professor at Duke University (2011, 445), have highlighted a dark side to creativity. Their evidence suggests that creative personalities who scored high on divergent thinking (a component of creativity) tended to cheat more on a problem-solving task. They also found the more creative the personality, the higher the level of dishonesty (2011, 449). Additionally, they say people who are creative or work in environments that promote creative thinking may be the most at risk of making unethical decisions when faced with ethical dilemmas (2011, 455).

Gino and Ariely's research has highlighted two striking differences between creativity and wisdom. Perhaps the most important differentiator between the creative and the wise is that creative pursuits and outcomes do not always have a moral basis, but an ethical concern is fundamental to wise actions.

The second key difference between the creative and the wise is personality. The creative personality is said to be ambitious and ardent; the wise personality, balanced and virtuous (Sternberg 2001). Creative individuals are often independent, determined, and passionate. Wise individuals have transcended self-centeredness and possess a well-integrated personality (Helson and Srivastava 2002, 1430).

I think there is a third significant difference that lies in motivation and, in consequence, how the time-horizon of solutions and consequences is considered. Creative individuals are motivated to demonstrate originality, innovation, and self-expression in the solutions they come up with. The wise are far more concerned with the longer-term ramifications of any solutions they might propose, and they will seek to find solutions and outcomes that most benefit all concerned. The creative value an evident originality over optimality. I have not found any reference to this as a differentiator in the academic literature I've reviewed, but perhaps it's out there somewhere.

What I have learned from researching the relationships among wisdom, intelligence, and creativity has confirmed my thinking about their interconnectedness and interrelatedness. I agree with Sternberg (1986) that all three have their uses, but it is especially wisdom that is needed to ensure we as a species not only continue to learn, grow, and flourish, but do so in ways that will benefit future generations.

WHY DOES WISDOM MATTER, AND WHY DO WE NEED IT?

"Without wisdom, any social or economic system is deficient because of the power of wisdom to provide good judgement, perspicacity, and ethically applied knowledge."
—ROONEY AND MCKENNA 2005, 308

Have you heard of the Fermi paradox? No? In 1950 over lunch with some colleagues, Enrico Fermi (Britannica), a physicist and Nobel Laureate, considered why we haven't seen any aliens. He is said to have asked, "But where is everybody?" given the size and age of the universe and the high probability of other life forms somewhere out there. Seventy years later, we're still wondering. One solution to this paradox is that any civilization, ours and others, has first to survive the consequences of its own technologies before setting off across the universe. If not managed effectively, the consequences of those technologies may drive the civilization to extinction before they can contact others.

How are we, Homo sapiens (wise man), doing so far? Let's consider two examples.

1. There is global consensus among scientists that an increase in carbon dioxide in the atmosphere of over 50 percent since the start of the Industrial Revolution in the mid-eighteenth century is adversely affecting our climate (NASA 2023; NOAA 2022). The planet is warming: weather systems are becoming destabilized and more chaotic; ice caps are melting; droughts, floods, and wildfires are becoming more frequent.

Politicians, through a series of compromises and treaties, are aiming to limit global temperature increase to 1.5 degrees Celsius (34.7 degrees Fahrenheit). But given it takes thousands of years for weather systems to reach stability, who really knows what this increase will look like?

2. Water is the basis of life on Earth, yet humanity allows chemical pollutants to enter water systems and oceans without due consideration of the effects and in pursuit of profits. For instance, micro-plastics have entered our food chains (Gerretsen 2023); so-called "forever chemicals," over 4,700 per- and poly-fluorinated alkyl substances, some known to be carcinogenic, are now ubiquitous. No one knows what the consequences will be (Schneider 2019).

These are not things that have happened sometime in the past. These are risks humanity is living with today and for the foreseeable future. The United Nations (UN) and its scientists are increasingly confident we face other equally significant challenges. These, they say, include: other issues arising from climate change such as ecosystem collapse, food shortages, and erosion of social cohesion; human population growth, overconsumption of resources, and infectious diseases; and short-termism among our policymakers, said by some to perhaps be the greatest threat for our future (WEF 2022; UNDP 2021).

The United Nations (UN) and its scientists are also increasingly concerned our politicians and policymakers are not addressing these issues with the seriousness and urgency they merit, with too much focus on optics and too little upon substance and implementation. But these are big, complex, interrelated, far-reaching, multi-generational problems. Could it be such problems require a different kind of "mind" to lead the search for solutions than those we have traditionally selected for the task?

The wise, as we have seen, are comfortable dealing with complexity, ambiguity, risk, and uncertainty. They take a dialectical view of issues; see multiple perspectives, interconnections and interdependencies. They look for solutions that balance the interests of multiple parties, considering the impact of actions and non-actions in both the short and the long-term. They do so with integrity and without self-interest.

So, back to the Fermi paradox. How are we doing so far in our efforts to survive the consequences of our technologies? Maybe not so well. Is there room for compromise? Can we survive irrationality and the failure to think long-term when facing potentially existential threats, or is there a place for selecting leaders and policymakers who exhibit much greater wisdom? The jury considering our performance may be out but not, I think, for long.

CHAPTER TWO

FROM THOUGHTS TO SCIENCE

When geriatric neuropsychiatrist Dr. Dilip V. Jeste compared the writings of an ancient Hindu text with modern Western definitions of wisdom, he made an astonishing discovery: they were almost identical.

Jeste was born and raised in India. As with many who live in Eastern cultures, he was accustomed to older people being respected and wise. He believes, "Unlike the modern Western societies where there's so much ageism, and people are considered a burden on the society, in Eastern cultures they are considered a great help. Families depend on them for advice."

Growing up in the Hindu religion, the Bhagavad Gita served as a sort of Bible, something that Jeste learned as a child growing up. The Bhagavad Gita, or Gita as it is more commonly called, is a 700-verse Hindu scripture which dates to the second half of the first millennium BC and is one of the sacred Hindu texts (Annenberg Lerner). He saw it as more than a book of religion but as a book on the philosophy of life and on wisdom. "So, you grow up thinking that there is such a thing as wisdom, you don't even think about this logically, you just say there is wisdom and older people are wiser, and you take those for granted."

Fueled by his love of reading, Jeste was fascinated by the works of Freud, which would eventually inspire him to study neuropsychiatry. But, during the 1970s, India offered limited opportunities to pursue the study of neuropsychiatry, so he moved to the US. He told me, "As a teenager, I was a bookworm, and I was most fascinated by Freud's books. I found that really understanding the mind and the brain is critical, because that's what Freud did. He was a neuropsychiatrist. He was not a psychiatrist only. He knew the brain and he said, 'Psychology rides on the back of physiology.' So, I said, 'This is what I'm going to do, to learn and research the brain and mind.' I went to medical school to become a psychiatrist. It was mostly the psychiatry part that attracted me to go into medicine. My research was on schizophrenia and serious mental illness."

Things got exciting when he was appointed as the director of the Stein Institute for Research on Aging at the University of California San Diego in 1986. "This was the first time," he said, "I got specifically interested in aging." He was studying aging and schizophrenia when he and his team stumbled on a remarkable finding.

Schizophrenia, usually regarded as a life sentence you never recover from, is also called "cancer of the mind"— things get progressively worse, and then you die.

Schizophrenia can reduce a person's lifespan by nearly fifteen years, not because the brain declines but because the patient fails to take care of other physical illnesses, such as diabetes, heart disease, stroke, and so on. However, Jeste and colleagues were astonished when they discovered the mental health of schizophrenics who survived into old age actually improved.

After copious experiments and numerous test subjects later, another surprise awaited Jeste and his team: "what I call 'the paradox of aging'; physical health declines and mental health improves. So, the next question is how can that happen biologically? The brain allows us to be happier with age when everything else deteriorates."

This got Jeste thinking. "Physical health is declining. Something must be happening to their brain and mind that makes them happier. They seem to develop more control over emotions as they got older. They are calmer and more self-reflective, and that made me wonder whether that is wisdom... since wisdom is associated with being more contented with life."

He was brought up to believe that "older people are wiser, and there is such a thing as wisdom. And I thought, is that something that can be scientifically proven?"

As an established professor of psychiatry who was well published, he started sounding out colleagues about the notion of doing research on wisdom, but they were less than supportive. He was told, "Nobody will take you seriously. It is not a scientific concept."

I have some sympathy with what Jeste encountered from his colleagues. When I was choosing a subject for my doctorate, I considered exploring the relationship between wisdom and leadership. One of my doctoral supervisors was not at all happy with this. She felt I would be subjecting my work to too much critique because psychological wisdom was not as well researched in 2002 as it is now in 2023. She felt the measurement of wisdom was not credible enough to incorporate in my doctoral work. After much debate, I decided to go with levels of psychological development instead of psychological wisdom.

The field of brain science has been dismissive of psychological and philosophical concepts, like consciousness and resilience. Wisdom has been similarly treated. But in Jeste's view, "If you want to do science, you must start by defining it and measuring it. If you can't define and measure it, you can't do science."

Then Jeste did something unconventional: He took the English translation of the ancient Hindu text, the Gita, to try to identify what the common characteristics of wise people were as opposed to foolish people. In effect, he used the Gita as a template to discern the competencies of wise behavior, noting very humorously, "The Gita was not written so that one day somebody would do scientific research with it."

What the research team found was astonishing. Most of the competencies derived from the Gita were identical to the modern definitions of wisdom, with two exceptions: divinity and religion, and anti-materialism, two aspects

the Gita focuses on but which are absent in modern definitions. According to Jeste, the definition of wisdom stays
largely similar in ancient philosophies across the world,
religions, and modern Western science.

"Wisdom bears the connotations of 'ancient' and seemingly transcends time, knowledge, and even culture.
All peoples, whether primitive or civilized, have sought
to pass their wisdom on to following generations by
means of myths, stories, songs, and even cave paint-
ings that date back 30,000 years," according to James E.
Birren, founder of the field of gerontology, and Cheryl
M. Svensson, instructor at the University of Southern
California (2005, 3).

The earliest "wisdom literature" is found on Sumerian
clay tablets, dating from more than 5,000 years. These set
out philosophical thoughts and contain practical advice
for everyday existence. The Egyptians thrived from 3200
BC to 300 AD and are credited with some of the earliest written wisdom teachings. These are believed to be
sources for the wisdom in the Torah and the books of the
Old Testament, used by both Judaism and Christianity
(Birren and Svensson 2005, 4).

It was the Greeks, the "lovers of wisdom," who were
the first philosophers to apply reason to the subject of
wisdom, as opposed to interpreting it through religion,
authority, and tradition. And, of all the ancient Greek
philosophers, no one changed the perception and understanding of wisdom more than Socrates (Birren and
Svensson 2005, 4).

SOCRATES

Socrates (470–399 BC) is considered an enigmatic character who, despite having penned none of the sayings or thoughts commonly attributed to him, is still regarded as one of very few philosophers who transformed the way philosophy and wisdom are thought about (Swartwood and Tiberius 2019, 11-12).

Everything we know about Socrates, what he said and did, comes from the writings of others, most notably his student and protégé, the philosopher Plato (428–348 BC). Socrates had a style of questioning, later termed the "Socratic method." It is defined as "a form of cooperative argumentative dialogue between individuals, based on asking and answering questions to stimulate critical thinking and to draw out ideas and underlying presuppositions" (Learning Without Scars 2020). It usually succeeds in demonstrating the limitations of knowledge. He advocated that everything should be questioned, nothing assumed. Throughout his lifetime, Socrates refused the notion that humans can be wise. He conceded only God is wise. Men could be "lovers of wisdom," but they could not be wise themselves (Birren and Svensson 2005, 5).

For Socrates, wisdom was epitomized by knowing what you do not know (or accepting the limitations of your own knowledge), a view which is held by philosophers and psychologists alike and often used as a yardstick to discern whether someone is wise or not. We can consider the way Socrates viewed his own "human wisdom" as a form of "epistemic humility"—an awareness of one's ignorance of the most important things, such as the nature of a good and virtuous life (Swartwood and Tiberius 2019, 11-12).

He spent much of his time in philosophical debates about how one ought to live. He found people who thought themselves to be wise and subjected their views to rational examination to see if they possessed the wisdom he hoped to find. Socrates made it clear his "human wisdom" was only valuable if it served to motivate the pursuit of another kind of wisdom: a deep understanding of the most important things (Swartwood and Tiberius 2019, 11-12).

It was Aristotle, mentored by Plato, who expanded on Socrates' notion of "the most important things."

ARISTOTLE

Aristotle (384-322 BC) furthered the understanding of wisdom by distinguishing between two types: one, theoretical wisdom ("sophia" in Greek), an understanding of the realities of the world; and two, practical wisdom ("phronesis" in Greek), a deep and comprehensive grasp of how we ought to live and conduct ourselves, of what is good and why (Swartwood 2022, 16). To become wise, Aristotle believed, individuals need to be of good (moral) character (Baltes and Smith 2008, 57).

Aristotle viewed theoretical wisdom as "the highest intellectual and philosophical excellence that a human mind is capable of achieving; it is a result of studying nature for its own sake, not for the sake of deliberation and action"

(Schwartz and Sharpe 2019, 227). Theoretical wisdom is concerned with unchanging truths, not with things that we can change. Practical wisdom is about the things we can change; to consider context and choices, then to take the right action (Schwartz and Sharpe 2019, 227).

For Aristotle, practical wisdom was the essence of wise action. It enabled an individual to draw from their theoretical knowledge and scientific understanding to apply these to concrete situations and dilemmas. Practical wisdom is essential to set priorities for action. This selection process is guided by intuition, values, and emotion (Baltes and Smith 2008, 57).

THE HEBREW PEOPLE

Socrates believed only God was wise, and man cannot be wise. However, when the Hebrew people took on board the concept of wisdom, they added a different theological spin on it. They believed not only does God possess wisdom, but he gives it to humanity as a gift, thereby adding a spiritual dimension to wisdom (Birren and Svensson 2005, 6).

The Hebrew people who voyaged from Samaria to Palestine in about 2200 BC transformed the way wisdom was perceived by the Greek philosophers. They believed wisdom was divine enlightenment and revelation of truth from God. The Hebrew Bible, the Torah, has several references to wisdom, particularly in the books of Job, Proverbs, and Ecclesiastes, which model aspirational behavior. The book of Proverbs also describes qualities of wisdom, which include, "The fear of the Lord is the beginning of wisdom" (Birren and Svensson 2005, 7). This seems to speak to a "spiritual dimension" often encountered among the wise (see chapter seven).

The Jewish king Solomon, who lived in the ninth century BC, was considered wise. His wisdom was believed to be a "divine gift from Yahweh, an exercise of justice, political wisdom, technical wisdom, intelligence, and knowledge." With the advent of Christianity, a greater differentiation was made between the earlier philosophic view of wisdom as a human quality at its most evolved and the concept of spiritual wisdom as a gift from God (Birren and Svensson 2005, 7).

ST. AUGUSTINE OF HIPPO

Under Christianity, all written philosophical works of Greek origin were scrutinized to ensure they were in keeping with Christian doctrine (Birren and Svensson, 7). St. Augustine of Hippo (354–430 AD) was one of the earliest to combine classical philosophical teachings with the notion of an omnipotent and omniscient God. He believed intelligence had two parts: "wisdom or sapientia, which is eternal, and scientia, the knowledge of the material world." Wisdom was regarded as moral perfection and the absence of sin. Augustine believed man's sinful nature hinders him from reaching the highest wisdom of God (Birren and Svensson 2005, 7).

Wisdom was emptied of its divinity when a certain young Indian man took a bold step, leaving everything of privilege to live a homeless, holy life in pursuit of what he saw as a higher purpose.

PRINCE SIDDHARTHA GAUTAMA

Prince Siddhartha Gautama was born (563–483 BC) into nobility in the village of Lumbini, now Nepal. He left his privileged life, wife, and son at age twenty-nine in search of a higher truth. Strange as it might seem, prior to that day, Gautama had never ventured outside the royal residence and, hence, had never witnessed suffering or poverty. When he was informed that sickness and death would befall him also, he abandoned his royal commitments to live as a homeless, holy man in search of a higher purpose (Jeste and LaFee 2020, 77–78). After his enlightenment under the Bodhi tree, he became known as the "Buddha" or "Awakened One" (Birren and Svensson 2005, 8). He taught by way of conversations and stories and focused on conduct and behavior rather than esoteric theology and practice. His teachings suggested that wisdom is "knowing something by personal observation and experience" (Birren and Svensson 2005, 8).

Our journey in our understanding of wisdom takes us from India to China, where the most influential Chinese philosopher and teacher profoundly impacted the civilizations of China and other East Asian countries.

CONFUCIUS

Considered the epitome of Chinese sages, Confucius (551–479 BC) is a Latin form of his Chinese name Kong Fuzi, meaning Master Kong (Yao 2000, 21). Confucius is believed to have been a descendant of the royal house of the Shang Dynasty. He was born in the state of Lu (now Shandong province), under the Zhou Dynasty, but was raised in poverty by his mother from the age of three after his father died (Britannica). He married at age nineteen and had a son and later two daughters, one of whom reportedly died as a child. Although Confucius grew up in poverty then worked initially in various modest positions, he was reported to have been an avid scholar and, in mid-life, was appointed minister of works then minister of crime (Britannica).

The Zhou Dynasty was based on a system of feudalism and espoused stability and pacifism. However, the dynasty collapsed, leading to great political instability, intense social unrest, military conflict, and competition over land and property. Whilst the rich continued to enjoy their extravagance, the poor were left destitute, prompting Confucius to consider how this could best be corrected (Yao 2000, 22).

Confucius reasoned society needed to change, to set goals to benefit the many rather than the few; that government should encourage morality and discipline, not impose cruel, punitive laws; that individuals should cultivate concern, compassion, and purity, and demonstrate goodness to others. He believed education and reflection were key to these transformations; that it was essential for those who were in, or aspired to, positions of authority to develop and display discipline and moral virtue. By these means, he argued, moral and social excellence, and a harmonious society, could be achieved (Yao 2000, 23).

The written work most closely associated with Confucius is the Analects, which was compiled by his disciples over the two or three centuries following his death. It is a collection of anecdotes and sayings which capture the core values of his thoughts. Interestingly, Confucius never thought himself an original thinker, saying, "I transmit but do not innovate" (Britannica).

Confucius said, "To know what you know and know what you don't know is the characteristic of one who knows" (Birren and Svensson 2005, 9).

The philosophies of East and West appear to converge on a universal concept of wisdom. They embrace the notion of focusing on what is good for the many rather than the few who are usually privileged in some way or another.

There has been a common thread on our journey through time to capture the essence of wisdom, from its earliest appearance in Egyptian hieroglyphics, its rationality in the Greek minds, its conception as a "divine gift" by Judaism and Christianity, through to Eastern moral instruction on how to live peaceably and demonstrate goodness to others. Wisdom has been portrayed and thought of as an ideal endpoint. "Wisdom is associated with good judgment and actions that contribute to living well" (Baltes and Smith 2008, 56).

G. Stanley Hall, pioneering psychologist and educator, is thought to be the first psychologist to write about the concept of wisdom in his book, *Senescence, the Last Half of Life*, published in 1922. He regarded the development of wisdom as "the emergence in later adulthood of a meditative attitude, philosophic calmness, impartiality, and the desire to draw moral lessons" (Staudinger and Glück 2011, 216).

WISDOM IN THE PSYCHOLOGICAL SCIENCES

Psychologist Gerard M. Brugman, who reviewed both the historical concepts and the psychological theories of wisdom, noted that "almost all central philosophical notions about wisdom have been incorporated in psychological theories" (Brugman 2006, 447). These notions include "assumptions about the meaning of life, virtue, and acknowledgment of human limitations" (Brugman 2006, 447–448), knowing what one does not know (or comprehending the limitations of one's own knowledge), and that the outcomes of wise actions or wise decisions benefit the many rather than simply a few. The psychological study of wisdom encompasses more than just wise people or wise behavior, it also includes the scrutiny of texts, such as religious writings, proverbs, and constitutional texts (Staudinger and Glück 2011, 216).

Two methods psychologists have used to inform their theorizing are implicit or subjective and explicit or expert theories. The early psychological theorizing was of the implicit kind, where lay people or non-experts who participated in psychological studies were asked to give an account of how they viewed a particular term, in this case, what they meant by "wisdom." This is followed up by explicit theorizing, where psychologists (or other professionals) reflect on the conceptions of laypeople, try to structure or categorize some of those thoughts, and add their own, producing more formal explicit theories of the psychological construct under discussion.

The doctoral research of Vivian Clayton, geriatric neuropsychologist, in 1976, inspired a number of psychological theories of wisdom and demonstrates the importance of incorporating "lay" or non-expert views in formulating and progressing theory (Birren and Svensson 2005, 19). Early studies, such as Clayton's, that looked at the layperson's conceptions of wisdom were the foundations on which explicit psychological theories developed. Explicit theories define and measure wisdom based upon the views of experts and other professionals. These experts then use empirical methods to differentiate those who are wise from those who are not, to investigate what other traits, characteristics, and environmental factors are related to wisdom (Glück 2022, 53).

The field of psychological wisdom has grown considerably over the past few decades. There are as many definitions of wisdom in the psychological wisdom literature as there are theories. For the sole purpose of our discussion, I will attempt to separate the body of work into two areas based on Ursula Staudinger's conception of personal versus general wisdom (Mickler and Staudinger 2009).

Those who have followed a "personal wisdom" approach usually have their origins in personality psychology, which culminates in wisdom depicted as the apex of human development or an ideal endpoint of personality growth. The scientific study of personal wisdom can be found in clinical, personality, and developmental psychology.

Two examples of theories that tend to fall more within the personal wisdom space are:

1. Monika Ardelt's three-dimensional wisdom scale (3DWS) and related model. She defines wisdom as a combination of personality characteristics with three broad components: cognitive, affective (compassion), and reflective (Ardelt 2003).

2. Jeffrey Dean Webster's self-assessed wisdom scale (SAWS) and HERO(E) model has five interrelated dimensions of wisdom, which need to operate together in a wise person in a holistic manner. These are: humor, emotion regulation, reminiscence and reflectiveness, openness, and critical life experiences (Webster 2007).

Those taking the more "general wisdom" route have stronger ties to philosophical wisdom literature, where wisdom is pictured as wise counsel or deep insight into life matters. The scientific study of general wisdom originated from cognitive research. The best-known example is the Berlin wisdom project.

THE BERLIN WISDOM PROJECT

The late Paul B. Baltes and his colleagues at the Max Planck Institute for Human Development, Berlin, Germany, established the project in the late 1980s. During his time at the Institute, Baltes trained and mentored numerous colleagues, many of whom are today's foremost wisdom researchers. The Berlin group has attempted to integrate philosophical concepts, with psychological theories and methods primarily from lifespan psychology and gerontology. They broadly define wisdom as "excellence in mind and virtue with a specific characterization of wisdom as an expert knowledge system dealing with the conduct and understanding of life" (Baltes and Smith 2008, 56).

As the first major explicit theory of wisdom, the Berlin group encountered much critique (and praise) with regard to defining and attempting to measure a complex and multidimensional construct like wisdom (Baltes and Smith 2008, 58; Sternberg 1998, 349).

THE STERNBERG CHRONICLES

Much like a conductor of an orchestra, Sternberg pulled together everyone who was anyone in the field of wisdom and orchestrated the publishing of the first edited book to combine contemporary empirical research on wisdom called *Wisdom: Its Nature, Origins, and Development* (1990). This book would serve as a source to many individuals desiring to further their knowledge, understanding, and research in wisdom.

Sternberg himself is the maestro of theories, which include intelligence, creativity, love, and wisdom. In his balance theory of wisdom, he emphasizes how wisdom is used in the world. He believes a wise person is someone who uses their personal qualities to benevolent ends. Decades later, Sternberg followed up his orchestral talent with several "handbooks" on wisdom. If you reviewed them, you would notice that, from the first in 2005 (Sternberg and Jordan) to the latest in 2019 (Sternberg and Glück), the number of contributors has increased substantially. The handbooks and content have become much more structured with each passing decade. Perhaps this clarity of presentation of material in some way shows how the field (the psychology of wisdom) has evolved.

It was in the 2019 *The Cambridge Handbook of Wisdom* that I first came across one of the edited chapters, titled "Neurobiology of Wisdom," that got me really excited about the scientific search for wisdom in the human brain. In this chapter, Dr. Dilip V. Jeste and Dr. Ellen E. Lee tell us where in the brain they found "wisdom" processing: "It is clear that the prefrontal cortex has a major role in the wisdom neurocircuitry" (Sternberg and Glück 2019, 77).

The prefrontal cortex (PFC), which is the newest part of the brain, consists of two parts: the lateral PFC (dorsolateral prefrontal cortex and ventrolateral prefrontal cortex) and the ventromedial PFC (also known as the orbitofrontal PFC). When wise people make benevolent decisions that require emotion regulation, balancing of apparently contradictory values, and managing ambiguity, they activate their lateral prefrontal cortex. This activation is particularly relevant when balancing self-interests with those of others, discussed in detail in chapter five. The medial prefrontal cortex is where empathy, compassion, and self-reflection are centered (Lee and Jeste 2019, 73).

In Jeste's book, *Wiser*, he discusses where the major components of wisdom processing are in the brain by way of a whistle-stop tour (Jeste and LaFee 2020, 19–26). For those of you who would like to learn a bit more, or just enjoy more neurobiology, I highly recommend his book.

What follows next is the explosive story of Phineas Gage, who is regarded as neuroscience's most famous patient.

NEUROSCIENCE OF WISDOM

In the afternoon of September 13, 1848, Phineas Gage's life took a horrific turn (Jeste and LaFee 2020, 30; Twomey 2010). Whilst clearing away rock to build the Rutland and Burlington Railroad near the town of Cavendish, Vermont, an iron rod shot through his skull. It entered his head just below his left cheek bone, passed behind his left eye, ripped through the lower portion of his brain's left frontal lobe, and exited through the top of his skull slightly behind his hairline. Miraculously, Gage did not even lose consciousness. He survived the ordeal but was not the same man after his injury.

Before the accident, Gage had been highly regarded, not only for his skills but also for being an upright and conscientious citizen. His physician, Dr. John Martyn Harlow, wrote of Gage: "Although untrained in the schools, he possessed a well-balanced mind, and was looked on by those who knew him as a shrewd, smart businessman, very energetic and persistent in executing all his plans of operation" (Jeste and LaFee 2020, 32).

After the railroad accident, Harlow wrote: "The balance between his intellectual faculties and animal propensities seemed gone. He could not stick to plans, uttered the grossest profanity and showed little deference for his fellows" (Twomey 2010). The primary area of Gage's brain damaged by the injury was the left frontal lobe. This is part of the pre-frontal cortex, which controls higher cognitive functions such as reasoning, learning, and complex decision making (Jeste and LaFee 2020, 21).

When I discussed Gage's case with Dr. Dilip V. Jeste, he observed that even though there might have been damage to one part of the brain, other parts are not completely unaffected. The brain works in an interconnected and interdependent way. Each part is connected to other parts, and so other parts of the brain suffer because their circuitry to the region is cut off. Interestingly, Jeste had found that wisdom processing is located in the exact area where Gage's brain was so severely damaged. Jeste was emphatic when he told me that Gage's "IQ was unaffected, providing yet further evidence that wisdom and intelligence are not the same things... there was, however, a distinct change in his personality from a disciplined to an unrestrained man."

Damage to the prefrontal cortex or to the limbic striatum have been found to cause specific behavioral and psychological changes that indicate a loss of multiple components of wisdom, such as prosocial behaviors, emotion regulation, and self-reflection (Lee and Jeste 2019, 73). This may well be what was observed by Gage's physician when he noted the deterioration of Gage's behavior: a lack of self-control, self-discipline, and, in particular, the inability to regulate his previously mild-mannered emotions.

The story of Phineas Gage and other similar cases have taught neurologists and neuropsychiatrists a great deal about how damage to certain areas of the brain is linked to specific changes in behavior. As Jeste put it, "There are other people who have damage to the occipital lobe, parietal lobe, that did not become unwise." However, they found, the damage occurred in the prefrontal cortex, and in some cases, in the amygdala as well, which are the areas of the brain that Jeste and his colleagues identified as those where wisdom processing is located.

So, the million-dollar question to Jeste is: If you can stimulate those regions where wisdom is located, can people become wiser? His answer: "I personally think yes, but the science has not yet advanced for us to be able to do so. Perhaps, in ten-, fifteen-, or twenty-years' time, there'll be ways in which we can stimulate specific parts of the brain without impacting other regions."

Research into the neurobiology of wisdom is the latest contribution to the study of wisdom. There is much to do in this area because we still know very little about the human brain. But, in the words of Jeste, "similarities between how wisdom was portrayed thousands of years ago in the Gita, in the West today, and in the story of Phineas Gage make you think it's not a cultural phenomenon but biologically based."

PART II

THE HALLMARKS OF WISDOM

CHAPTER THREE

EXTENDING COGNITION

Do you know about the devasting, man-made medical disaster of the late fifties, early sixties affecting the babies of thousands of pregnant women in almost fifty countries (Science Museum 2019)? Have you heard of a drug called thalidomide? It provided pregnant women with relief from the dreaded morning sickness but, unbeknownst to them, put them at high risk of giving birth to infants with severe disabilities.

Thalidomide was responsible for more than ten thousand babies born with a range of disabilities, which included malformation of limbs, hands, and fingers; sensory impairment; and damage to the brain, internal organs, and skeletal structure (Science Museum 2019). One woman's decision to refuse FDA approval of the drug reduced thalidomide's impact in the US and might have caused others to reconsider the drug's safety (Bren 2001).

Originally introduced in 1953 as a sedative or tranquilizer to facilitate sleep, thalidomide was found effective in the treatment of a wide range of other conditions, including some forms of leprosy, colds, flu, nausea, and morning sickness (Bren 2001).

The drug's German manufacturer claimed it was "non-addictive and was safe for pregnant women" (Bren 2001). By 1957, thalidomide was available without a prescription in Germany. By 1960, it was sold throughout Canada, Europe, South America, and in many other parts of the world. To introduce thalidomide into the United States, the Richardson-Merrell pharmaceutical company of Cincinnati applied for FDA approval in September 1960 (Bren 2001).

The application was assigned to medical officer Frances Oldham Kelsey, who had joined the FDA just one month earlier. It was her first drug review assignment. At the outset, Kelsey, as well as the pharmacologist and chemist who assisted her, had several concerns about the drug. Detailing these deficiencies in a letter to Richardson-Merrell, the company's response was less than satisfactory. Kelsey noted, "The clinical reports were more on the nature of testimonials rather than the results of well-designed, well-executed studies" (Bren 2001).

Kelsey continued to request more data about the drug's safety, exasperating Dr. Joseph Murray, Richardson-Merrell's representative, who repeatedly called and visited Kelsey to expedite matters. He complained to her superiors that she "was unreasonable and nit-picking, and... was delaying the drug's approval unnecessarily." But Kelsey did not give way to the pressure (Bren 2001).

"I think I always accepted the fact that one was going to get bullied and pressured by industry," said Kelsey. Richardson-Merrell continued to harass her and, because their attempts were unsuccessful, they eventually owned up and said, "We want to get this drug on the market before Christmas, because that is when our best sales are" (Bren 2001).

In December of 1960, three months after Richardson-Merrell submitted its application, the *British Medical Journal* published a letter from a physician, Alexander Leslie Florence, who had prescribed thalidomide to his patients. Florence described his concerns after noticing several neurological-related problems in those patients who had taken the drug over a long period of time. Those patients who stopped taking the drug noticed an improvement in their conditions. After reading Florence's letter, Kelsey immediately contacted Richardson-Merrell to ask for additional information on these side effects (Bren 2001).

Previously, she had seen the effects of quinine (a medication used to treat malaria and some bovine diseases) on the fetuses of rabbits and wondered whether thalidomide might affect the developing human fetus, suspecting that a drug that could damage nerves in adults could also affect babies in the womb.

Her concerns soon proved to be valid. Her repeated request for more data, which prevented the approval of thalidomide, did more than just keep a dangerous drug off the US market. She set into motion a series of events that would forever change the way drugs are tested, evaluated, and introduced in America, prompting other countries to apply similar standards.

As the drug was traded under so many different names in different countries, it took five years for the connection between thalidomide taken by pregnant women and the impact on their babies to be made. The first time the link between thalidomide and its impact on fetal development was made public was in a letter published by the Australian obstetrician William McBride in *The Lancet* in 1961. McBride wrote he had observed "multiple severe abnormalities" in babies whose mothers had taken thalidomide during pregnancy. He concluded his letter by asking: "Have any of your readers seen similar abnormalities in babies delivered of women who have taken this drug during pregnancy?" The drug was formally withdrawn by the German manufacturer on November 26, 1961, and by UK distributors a few days later on December 2, 1961 (Science Museum 2019).

Later in this chapter I will discuss how wise people push generally accepted standards to beyond the conventional, possibly even creating meta-standards that redefine what is possible or acceptable. Kelsey's actions in the FDA evaluation of thalidomide, and the changes this precipitated, fall squarely into the latter.

Robert J. Sternberg, professor of human development at Cornell University, asserts in his balance theory of wisdom that a person is wise to the extent they use their skills and knowledge to achieve a common good

(Sternberg 1998; Sternberg, Glück, and Karami 2022, 55). To do this, he says, they must balance their own, larger, and others' interests over the long-term and short-term, through the utilization of positive ethical values, by adapting to, shaping, and selecting environments (Sternberg 1998; Sternberg, Glück, and Karami 2022, 55).

For Sternberg, achieving a common good means "attaining a goal that benefits all of the parties who are affected by a judgment or decision, including people who have interests different from one's own" (Sternberg, Glück, and Karami 2022, 55). He believes it's a real challenge for people to behave wisely because of their tendency to focus on short-term benefits at the expense of long-term advancements.

Richardson-Merrell's focus was short-term—on the profits that thalidomide would generate over the Christmas period. Kelsey, on the other hand, was concerned about the babies who might potentially be at risk, their mothers, their families, and their futures.

The thalidomide dilemma required a solution that demonstrated a balance of cognitive, emotional, and moral components, intricately interwoven to consider the benefits to each of the parties affected by the judgment or decision. It seems Kelsey's final verdict took into consideration the "common good" (Sternberg, Glück, and Karami 2022, 55) and, whilst probably not part of Kelsey's considerations and not appreciated by Richardson-Merrell at the time, likely saved Richardson-Merrell from costly court cases, loss of reputation, and millions of dollars in damages.

Kelsey may have been intimidated but chose to ignore the complaints the drug-house made to her superiors about her thoroughness, which they regarded as unnecessarily delaying approval. If we place Kelsey's actions within the framework of Sternberg's theory, then she was committed to the common good, stayed focused on her larger ethical values (to keep a dangerous drug off the market), and realized the long-range consequences of her decision could potentially impact generations of mothers, babies, families, communities, and so on.

Few can doubt the need for wisdom in addressing an issue with a global health impact, but is it, you may ask, needed to solve everyday, ordinary problems?

Ute Kunzmann, professor of life-span developmental psychology, Leipzig University, Germany (2022, 157), has suggested wisdom is needed when one is faced with a problem where no clear-cut solution is available. Perhaps, the problem has not been fully diagnosed or understood, is emotionally charged, and will involve multiple persons, all of whom have concerns, agendas, and motives pertaining to certain outcomes. There is further consensus that, in those intractable life situations that most require wisdom, a balance of cognitive, emotional, moral, reflective, and other components operate in unison and synchronicity (Glück and Weststrate 2022, 2).

This, however, is an academic analysis and begs two all-important questions in real-world situations. First, would someone who is not wise recognize they were facing such a problem? Second, if so, would they be prepared to admit the problem was beyond their competence?

Oftentimes, the consequences of decisions taken by people in positions of power are like the ripples in a pond. Such decisions have the potential to impact communities, societies, countries, and the world. The issue is not so much that a problem has no clear-cut solution, but rather the people who have taken, or who will take, action seem not always to consider, or perhaps are not capable of, considering the ramifications of their actions. Those who do consider the longer-range consequences will most likely take decisions that benefit the largest number of people.

The ability to embrace contradictory aspects of an issue, to consider and accept opposing viewpoints, and to change one's opinion on a matter when faced with new information is enabled by dialectical thinking (Kramer 1990). Those who have written extensively about wisdom agree it is the wise individual's ability to think dialectically that enables wise judgments and prudent decisions that consider the longer-range consequences (Sternberg 2001; Kramer 1990).

DIALECTICAL THINKING

Michael Basseches, professor emeritus of psychology, Suffolk University, Boston, provided insight into the use of dialectical thinking as an advanced form of adult cognitive functioning. Dialectical thinking, or a dialectical worldview, assumes everything is interrelated, interconnected, and all things are constantly transforming: "old forms give way to new emergent forms" (Basseches 1984, 404).

Underlying the development of dialectical thinking is the notion that adults develop through challenges that upset existing beliefs and understanding. Such challenges, like the thalidomide dilemma, often present as ill-structured problems that have multiple causes and effects and where multiple perspectives and conflicting notions about what the best course of action is must be considered. Basseches suggests that, as dialectical thinking emerges, the individual increasingly considers and takes responsibility for their own actions and beliefs (1984).

When I was conducting the interviews for my doctoral work, one of the female leaders, Sally, stood out from the rest as an excellent example of someone with the capacity for dialectical thinking.

In my research, I used several tests to assess the level of psychological development (cognitive, emotional, and moral) of each participant. From the main sample, I randomly selected a sub-sample to interview. Sally happened to be one of them. To those leaders whom I interviewed I gave a test (Wonderlic Personnel Test 2002) to assess their level of cognitive complexity (their ability to solve complex problems, speed of processing, and abstract thinking). This test was timed and scored by the number of correct answers within the time limit (twelve minutes for fifty questions). At the time of the interviews, I had all the results from the psychological test battery, so I knew Sally scored in the top percentile for emotional and moral maturity.

Of the interview questions, the final four were aimed at assessing their dialectical thinking ability. I was assessing whether they demonstrated:

- the ability to see multiple perspectives and make connections among these,
- the ability to consider the long-range consequences of their decisions,
- whether their thoughts reflected interdependence rather than independence,
- an acceptance of contradiction and ambiguity when dealing with complex issues, and
- a recognition that things are constantly evolving and transforming.

The way in which Sally answered the final four questions reflected her ability to see systems as open and how each is part of larger systems. She was able to understand and acknowledge her role as a variable and active component in the larger process and to take responsibility as an "active constructor of experience," rather than passively reacting to it (Kramer 1990, 280). The breadth and depth of her reasoning, her levels of abstraction, and her ability to make connections between and among things was impressive. Remember the cognitive complexity test, which was given only to interview participants? Well, I was delighted but unsurprised to discover Sally received an almost perfect score on the test and the highest, by far, in my sample. Sally scored forty-eight out of fifty (the average score for senior executives on this test is twenty-eight).

Wisdom researchers Judith Glück and Nic M. Weststrate observed that wise people seek an unbiased appreciation of the problem or issue; consider the problem and pathways to possible solutions, guided by ethical principles to optimize a common good; and propose or implement the best possible solution (Glück and Weststrate 2022, 3). What really resonates with me from among the many significant points they make in this article is their suggestion that wise decisions do not necessarily need a positive outcome.

"The world we have made, as a result of the thinking we have done thus far, creates problems we cannot solve at the same level of thinking at which we created them."
—ALBERT EINSTEIN, PHYSICIST AND NOBEL LAUREATE

What if we were able to anticipate problems before they were fully formed?

FINDING THE PROBLEM

The late psychologist, Patricia Kennedy Arlin, was a pioneer in uncovering the striking similarities between wisdom and problem finding (Arlin 1990, 230). One crucial similarity is the role of questions. Wisdom, she believes, is found more in the quality of questions posed than in the solutions derived from them. Wisdom and problem finding are not the same thing. One can be a problem finder and not be wise, but it is unlikely a wise person lacks a problem-finding ability. Wise people's questions will almost certainly lead to further questions. Arlin maintained that answers are to problem solving as questions are to problem finding, and the caliber of solutions derived is directly related to the caliber of questions asked (Arlin 1990, 231).

James T. Dillon, professor emeritus, University of California, Riverside, commented on the lack of research into problem finding. He observes that those who have written about the components of problem finding have referred to finding as discovering, formulating, or posing a problem; other terms used include problem sensing, problem formulation, and creative problem-discovering (Dillon 1983, 97–98).

The late Jacob W. Getzels, psychologist, educator, and leading figure on the study of creativity, was one of the pioneers to pursue problem finding as an area of empirical research. He said, "The question that is asked is the forerunner to the quality of the solution that will be attained" (Getzels 1982, 38). To illustrate his point, Getzels (1982, 38–39) uses a simple scenario:

The occupants of a car that blows a tire on a deserted country road find the jack is missing from the trunk. They define the problem as "Where can we get a jack?," recall they had passed a service station some miles back, and decide to walk there to get a jack. Whilst they are gone, along comes another car. It, too, blows a tire, and the occupants discover they don't have a jack. But they define the problem as: "How can we raise the car?" They notice a barn near the road where they discover a pulley for lifting hay bales. They push the car to the barn, lift it with the pulley, change the tire, and continue on their journey, whilst the occupants of the first car are still walking toward the service station.

Was this a clever solution, or was it a case of asking the right question?

"You can tell whether a man is clever by his answers. You can tell whether a man is wise by his questions."

—NAGUIB MAHFOUZ, EGYPTIAN WRITER
AND NOBEL PRIZE LAUREATE

A strong advocate of the belief that problem finding is a more significant activity than problem solving was Norman H. Mackworth, a psychologist and cognitive scientist, who used problem finding to describe his concept of originality in science (Arlin 1990, 232). He suggested that problem finding is what true scientists engage in, whereas complex problem solving is the domain of technical experts. Mackworth believed ill-defined problems, rather than well-structured problems, are the stimuli for problem finding. In problem finding, "it is a rather exacting requirement to have to work back from an unknown point or to have to simplify the mismatch between present position and an unknown destination" (Mackworth in Arlin 1990, 232).

Max Wertheimer, one of the three founders of Gestalt psychology, said, "The function of thinking is not just solving an actual problem but discovering, envisaging, going into deeper questions. Often, in great discovery, the most important thing is that a certain question is found" (Wertheimer in Arlin 1990, 232).

Wise people ask penetrating questions to reveal the heart of issues. Because wise people love learning, they seek to fully understand an issue, not rush to solution-mode prematurely. Going into deeper questions seems more like an adventure to them than a cognitive activity. It might be that the wise person's endless curiosity contributes to their pursuit of deeper levels of questioning and their insatiable desire to want to learn continuously.

Wisdom, like problem finding, is about the individual's willingness to remain open to receive new information and, based on that information, to be flexible and comfortable changing their worldview. But problem finding is only one aspect of wise behavior. Wise people often also push the boundaries of convention to new levels.

PUSHING THE LIMITS—META-STANDARDS

Researchers agree that wisdom is activated when a problem or dilemma is considered ill-defined or intractable, no single solution path is identifiable, and multiple constituents are invested in the outcome. Arlin reminds us, "When there is no known solution to a problem, the solution cannot be compared against a previous standard" (Arlin 1990, 233).

Decisions, judgments, or solutions are often deemed wise when they push generally accepted standards beyond the conventional to create new or meta-standards and, in so doing, redefine what is acceptable or possible (Arlin 1990, 233). One such example is the story of King Solomon, who solved the problem of two women who both claimed one baby as their own.

There were two women living in the same house. The first woman gave birth to a baby boy and, three days later, the other woman also had a baby boy. No one was in the house but the two of them. During the night the second woman's son died because she accidentally laid on him. So, she got up and exchanged her dead son with the first woman's son. The following morning, when the first woman got up to nurse her son, she discovered he was dead. But when she looked more closely at him in the morning light, she noticed it wasn't her son. Their dispute over the living baby led them to seek King Solomon's judgment.

When they were in the presence of the king, they continued arguing about whom the living baby belonged to. Eventually, the king asked for a sword to be brought and gave an order for the living child to be cut in two, giving half to one woman and half to the other. The true mother, out of love for her son, said to the king, "Please, my lord, give her the living baby! Don't kill him!" The second woman did not contest the ruling, declaring if she could not have the baby then neither of them could. "Then the king gave his ruling: 'Give the living baby to the first woman. Do not kill him; she is his mother'" (1 Kings 3:27, NIV).

Clayton says of Solomon's ruling that his solution seemed to lack rationality but reflected a clear understanding of human nature. The biological mother's plea upon hearing Solomon's judgment determined who the real mother was. Note also, at the heart of Solomon's solution was an apparent contradiction: in the face of a request to preserve life, his solution proposed extinction of life (Clayton 1982, 317).

The story of King Solomon's judgment seems dramatic, if not barbaric. But remember, it is written from the viewpoint of observers, not from Solomon's, and it's his that we should consider. Remember, too, the difference between ordinary and wise advice and solutions is marked. I like to think Solomon defined the problem along the lines of, "How do I identify the real mother without harming the baby?" Wise people see problems from multiple perspectives, and as a result they see more than one solution to most problems. The story we are told shows us, I think, that Solomon's first attempt to identify the real mother worked. I very much doubt Solomon ever intended to have the baby cut in half, and I have little doubt that, had he failed with his first attempt, he would have moved on to others until he succeeded. When the true mother screamed, and the assembled crowd gasped, I like to imagine Solomon smiled to himself and thought, *Well, that was a lot easier than I expected!*

Researchers widely accept that the presence of ill-defined problems that have no clear-cut solution activates wisdom. Complex problems require solutions that demonstrate a balance of cognitive, emotional, and moral components operating together. The wise person's dialectical worldview enables them to see more perspectives, make connections between and among these perspectives, and open to accept seemingly opposing viewpoints. This worldview allows them to be flexible and not dogmatic; to have no fixed views on things but to seek new information and practice fluidity of thought. Wise people take time to ask questions to better comprehend a problem and don't rush to solution. They are not bound by the status quo and may devise something completely different. This is why a wise person's advice can be so very different to what others might suggest.

CHAPTER FOUR

UNDERSTANDING EMOTION

I'll never forget April 27, 1994. I went to vote in the general elections for the first time in my life. I was already in my twenties. People of color were not previously permitted by law to vote.

Although I'm not usually overtly emotional in public, I couldn't stop the tears from flowing down my cheeks as I got into my car to travel to the nearest polling station. It was as though I had been set free, affirmed of my humanity, and, perhaps like many other people of color that day, for the first time in my life I felt truly proud to be South African. This day would forever change the political landscape of South Africa. It also changed the way I felt about my nationality.

The year 1994 was momentous for South Africa. The apartheid regime had finally toppled, and Nelson Rolihlahla Mandela became the first black president of South Africa. Mandela had spent many dreadful years in prison for his actions in pursuit of black emancipation, yet when he became president, he did not use the power of that office in pursuit of retribution and revenge. Instead, he chose forgiveness and looked for a way to unify all the peoples of South Africa as the "Rainbow Nation." Somehow, he identified the Rugby World Cup, due to be hosted by South Africa in 1995, as a vehicle to unification. Rugby was very much the white man's sport. Blacks favored football (or soccer).

Mandela asked to meet Francois Pienaar, the white captain of South Africa's team—the Springboks. Pienaar was astonished to meet Mandela, the more so when Mandela asked what it would take for South Africa to win the World Cup. The Springboks did not compete in the first two World Cups in 1987 and 1991 because of international anti-apartheid sporting boycotts (Rugby Rucker 2022). Mandela set in motion a process that led the entire South African nation to unify in support of the Springboks and, ultimately, to the Springboks winning the World Cup against all odds.

When Pienaar was interviewed (Pienaar 2013) about his relationship with Mandela, whom he fondly referred to as "Madiba" (Mandela's Xhosa clan name), he said, "It's just his presence and his aura, his selflessness, his humility... that package is powerful. He makes you feel that you can run faster, that you can jump higher." It was more than evident Nelson Mandela had left an indelible mark on Pienaar's life. Mandela became a symbol of peace and reconciliation, recognized the world over.

This story of Nelson Mandela could have turned out so differently. He could have emerged from his seven-by-nine-foot Robben Island cell (Johnson 2012) with a mission to overthrow a regime that had robbed him of twenty-seven years of his life. What was it that inspired Mandela to forgive his oppressors? Why did he not seek retribution?

When Mandela was interviewed by Canadian Broadcasting Corporation's Barbara Frum (CBC 2013), she asked him: "Where do you put any bitterness, and where do you put that human appetite for satisfaction, if not revenge?"

He answered, "Well, it's not easy if you are busy with constructive work to think about issues which make you bitter, and bitterness comes very easily when one is idle and has nothing to do. If you're busy with something positive, constructive, and rewarding, you are likely to forget experiences which have been counterproductive."

Actor Morgan Freeman, who played Mandela in the film *Invictus*, was asked by journalist Charlie Rose (December 6, 2013) about his starring role, and he said to play someone you need to know "how much energy is needed to be that person. And with Mandela, it's a very low energy ebb; he's very quiet inside... He's commanding; he has a most commanding presence, without being lordly..."

From several Mandela interviews I have listened to, I noticed he answered many of the questions with a "yes and no." When Barbara Frum (1990) asked him: "To the world you won a great war, but was the personal cost too high?" his answer was: "Well, yes and no. Yes, because to spend twenty-seven years in prison is too high a cost, especially when you have a family. But no, in the sense that as a result of this our attitude, our spirit, has been enriched, and we've had the opportunity of sitting down and reflecting on issues, and also the experience has gained us a lot of support locally and abroad, which perhaps we would not have gotten."

The way Mandela answered this question takes one from the personal to a much broader issue, the support for the abandonment of apartheid generated in South Africa and beyond. His answers to questions always gave the impression he kept his eye on the bigger picture. Yes, he was separated from his family, but consideration of what South Africa and the world would gain was perhaps of higher value to him in the final analysis.

Mandela, it seems, from his interview with Barbara Frum, had made his personal feelings subordinate to a vision of unification of former oppressor and oppressed. At a cognitive level, this took foresight, but I don't think that cognition alone would have driven Mandela's decision to forgo retribution. The decision must have involved emotion. After all, when he was released, a free man at last, he had tremendous power that he chose to use benevolently to affect the transformation of a country.

Mandela is regarded the world over as an exemplar of wise behavior. Wisdom exemplars have devoted themselves to helping others and have achieved major positive changes. Their benevolence is directed toward humanity and the world at large, as they seek to resolve complex situations in ways that balance gains and losses for all involved (Glück and Sternberg 2022, 126).

EMOTION AND COGNITION: SEPARATE OR INSEPARABLE?

The Stoic philosopher Seneca thought wisdom was only possible if reason dominated and emotions were silenced. David Hume, the eighteenth-century Scottish Enlightenment philosopher, in contrast, believed "reason is, and ought only to be, the slave of the passions" (Gross 1998, 287). Robert C. Solomon, philosopher and business ethicist, argued that wisdom is "the harmony of reason and the passions" (Gross 1998, 271).

Throughout history, there has been some dispute about the primacy of cognition over emotion and vice versa. However, decades of research have shown that neither operates in isolation of the other. Cognition influences emotion in areas such as attributions and appraisals, and emotion influences cognition in areas such as learning, attention, and memory (Callahan, Hasler, and Tolson 2005).

This beneficial intertwining of cognition and emotion is illustrated graphically by the words of António Damásio, professor of psychology, philosophy, and neurology at the University of Southern California: "When emotion is entirely left out of the reasoning picture, as happens in certain neurological conditions, reason turns out to be even more flawed than when emotion plays bad tricks on our decisions" (1994, 30).

Emotions are woven into every aspect of human life, from the moment of birth till the end of life. Not only are emotions integral to our sense or lack of well-being, they are also the foremost creators of self-interest, motivation, and the will to survive. Emotions influence thinking by motivating thought and information selection and, in some, reflection. They make us want certain things, and they direct our attention to some things and not to others. Emotions enhance one's perception and understanding of events, other people, and the world in general (Cassell 2002; Michie and Gooty 2005).

Clinical psychologist Deirdre Kramer (1990, 281) believes cognition and emotion interact with each other to produce a number of wisdom-related skills, which then manifest in the individual as they advise others or make important life decisions. Researchers, using functional MRI to seek evidence for an integration of emotion and cognition in the brain, found that "at some point of processing, functional specialization is lost, and emotion and cognition conjointly and equally contribute to the control of thought and behaviour" (Gray, Braver, and Raichle 2002, 4115). These cognitive and affective processes interact in wise behavior and may develop synergistically with practice and over time (Glück and Weststrate 2022).

I view cognition and emotion as two sides of a coin, linked one to the other, and the more psychologically evolved one becomes, the more integrated these processes become. The relationship between cognition and emotion is complex and still more so in the behavior of the wise.

EMOTIONAL COMPLEXITY

In chapter one, I spoke about one of my mentors, Eileen, whom I consider to be wise. One of the reasons I say this about her is because of her ability to access a broad range of emotional experiences that are finely differentiated. Sometimes, when she's describing something that happened to her, it's as though she's taking me on a tour of her emotions. We visit each one like a city. She describes how she felt with depth and diversity, and then she moves on as though she herself was just visiting, looking in from the outside. This impacts how she describes the emotions of others. What I find particularly fascinating about Eileen is not her depth of emotional experience but how she could be dealing with something quite traumatic in her own family, yet the focus of her conversation inevitably moves toward the person she's speaking to, in this case, me. She shifts her conversation to inquire how I am, what's going on in my life, desiring rather to listen to any difficulties I might be experiencing, demonstrating empathy and compassion toward my situation rather than seeking them from me.

In a similar vein, Morgan Freeman, in the interview with Charlie Rose, spoke of Mandela's empathy and compassion toward the prison guards: "So, he hears that a guard's child is sick. The guard comes to work, and he says, 'Good morning. How is your baby? Is she all right today?' Things like that." It seems wise people can defer their own needs to attend to the needs of others.

Wise people seem to have an inner serenity which allows them to operate along the continuum of negative to positive emotions without becoming overwhelmed by them, as did Mandela. "It may well be that openness to and competence in processing emotional information is the feature that distinguishes wisdom from intelligence or mere cleverness and permits the 'penetrating insights' and 'exceptional understanding' associated with wise people" (Lyster 1996, 26).

Emotional complexity is defined as having a broad range of well differentiated emotional experiences and the ability to view them from multiple perspectives. At the highest levels of emotional development, individuals see more perspectives, interconnections, and interrelations among things; are able to display empathy, equanimity, and embrace contradictory emotions; and become increasingly able to deal with uncertainty, ambiguity, and change. Emotional complexity is associated with individuals who are more attentive to their inner feelings and thoughts and open to experience (Kang and Shaver 2004, 717).

Furthermore, wise people seem particularly good at acknowledging and differentiating their emotions, then managing them to appropriate intensities. "Besides facilitating thoughtful consideration of life's problems, qualities such as patience and a sense of humor may be emotionally adaptive in coping with life crises and losses" (Lyster 1996, 28). Could it be wise people use humor as an empathic tool to reframe the way others perceive problems, thereby changing their emotional and cognitive perspectives?

Blake Bromley, international charity lawyer, wrote an article on "The Humor of Nelson Mandela." Blake met Mandela in 1995 and said, "Nelson Mandela was as humble and self-deprecating in person as he is portrayed in the media. He also radiated an awesome sense of presence. My dominant memory, however, is of his humor... He used humor as a subtle tool to diffuse confrontations before they turned ugly or violent. But he was not content to simply diffuse tension: He seized the opportunity, while people were still laughing, to make an unmistakable rebuke or a bald challenge to the perspective being promoted before the laughter began."

Jeffrey Dean Webster, professor of psychology, Langara College, Canada, is a wisdom researcher who believes humor is a component of wisdom. He believes humor derives from a combination of cognitive flexibility, openness to new ideas, and playfulness. He further believes that wise humor can be used to build and support emotional bonds with others; to recognize and illustrate irony, contradiction, and uncertainty; and to de-emphasize, even ridicule, certain points of view. It can also be used to show that one doesn't, and shouldn't, take oneself over-seriously (Webster 2007).

Emotions strongly impact how we perceive, interpret, and interact with others, events, and the world, but our emotions can sometimes be inappropriate or of such intensity that they hinder us. We are all equipped, to varying degrees, with the ability to manage our emotional responses. This ability is termed "emotion regulation."

EMOTION REGULATION

Emotion regulation refers to the "processes by which we influence which emotions we have, when we have them, and how we experience and express them" (Gross 2003, 282). Such processes, says James Gross, professor of psychology at Stanford University and director of the Stanford Psychophysiology Laboratory, may be automatic or controlled, conscious or unconscious. He suggests "a continuum from conscious, effortful, and controlled regulation to unconscious, effortless, and automatic regulation" (Gross 1998, 275). What I like about Gross' continuum is the sense of evolution. We can improve and enhance our capacities to regulate our emotions. They start out controlling us, and with discipline and effort, we can learn to manage our emotions until the process of regulation becomes increasingly unconscious.

When individuals regulate their emotions wisely, they do not ignore or suppress unwanted or inappropriate feelings. Rather, they acknowledge and accept their own feelings and those of others (Glück 2022, 183). It is not that they are emotionally detached from events; rather, they are not swamped by emotions and are able to maintain a reflective disposition in evaluating and generating responses (Birren and Fisher 1990, 321). A panel of wisdom researchers have identified emotion regulation as a crucial aspect of wise behavior (Jeste, Ardelt, Blazer, Kraemer, Vaillant, and Meeks 2010).

Wisdom researchers have found that wise individuals typically display equanimity and peace of mind. Although they will show a caring and empathic attitude toward those in distress, they tend to remain calm and take a broad, balanced, and objective view of the situation to provide effective help or advice to others.

Roger N. Walsh, professor of psychiatry, philosophy, and anthropology at the University of California, Irvine, defines the ability to "experience provocative stimuli fully and non-defensively without psychological disturbance" as equanimity (Walsh 2015, 289). Aurobindo (1872-1950), one of India's greatest philosophers and widely regarded as a sage, described equanimity as "the characteristic temperament of the sage" (Walsh 2015, 289).

Wisdom researcher Monika Ardelt conducted an exploratory study to test how wise people cope with crises and obstacles in their lives, revealing they use "higher-order or meta-strategies." One such strategy is "mental distancing": taking a step back to calm down, reflecting on the situation, and taking time to objectively consider and think about the problem from an emotional distance (Ardelt 2005, 11).

One of the wise individuals interviewed for Ardelt's (2005, 11) study, "James," was also described as the most reflective of all the research participants. This is how he described his response to adversity:

> *Normally, when something comes up that I'm unhappy about, the first thing I do is completely relax... and say to myself, I'll get through it... Usually, if I'll relax and give whatever the problem is some thought—don't try to solve it right then, just give it some thought, and*

it'll come to me. I don't know how, but it'll just come
to me and work itself out. But the thing is not to get
frustrated over it.

Two things are apparent from the way in which James
regulates his emotions. First, he manages to attain a sense
of calm in the face of adversity, a very important step
for what comes next. Second, he reflects on the problem,
giving it distance and space. This second part provides
opportunity for further insights to look at the problem
from different perspectives. Ardelt suggests one can grow
in self-awareness and self-insight by engaging in self-examination, developing greater objectivity, and gaining a
more compassionate understanding of oneself and others.
Through this one gains a deeper comprehension of human
nature. One's focus shifts from self to others, and, in so
doing, a greater motivation to help others in need evolves
(Ardelt and Jeste 2018, 1375).

One of the things I've noticed from observing wise people is that they tend to focus on others and how others
might be feeling. I mentioned earlier in this chapter how
Eileen paid attention to what I was experiencing rather
than seeking empathy and compassion for her own
problems. Perhaps it is that wise people have learned
over time to respond to adversity by regulating their
emotions, not trying to solve a problem in haste, and
somehow, as James put it, have confidence it will "work
itself out" (Ardelt 2005, 11).

EMPATHY, COMPASSION, AND ALTRUISM

Empathy is defined as "an affective state that stems from the apprehension of another's emotional state or condition, and that is congruent with it. Thus, empathy can include emotional matching and the vicarious experiencing of a range of emotions consistent with those of others" (Eisenberg and Miller 1987, 91).

Researchers have suggested that empathy has two components. The first, cognitive empathy, is the ability to accurately gauge what another is feeling. It is understanding what caused the person's emotional state. This gives individuals access to relevant information about the situation and the people involved. The second is emotional empathy, sharing another person's feelings. This component must be practiced with care, as it may constrain a person's ability to see the broader picture and consider other perspectives (Glück and Weststrate 2022, 18).

The positive effects of demonstrating empathy were expressed with eloquence by Cooper and Sawaf (1997, 51): "Through feelings of empathy and compassion we help ourselves learn and grow, and we also enable others to begin to feel safe enough to talk about what is really going on in their lives—to tell their stories—without fear of being judged or criticized."

Cooper and Sawaf touch on something rather pertinent, feeling safe to be one's authentic self "without fear of being judged or criticized," which lies at the heart of how wise people respond to the challenges of others. They do not judge or criticize others, but rather show compassion toward what the person might be feeling and experiencing. They have a way of making others feel they can be trusted. Deirdre Kramer described the wise person's behavior as "particularly adept at taking the perspective of others and providing a safe setting in which others can explore their own values, thoughts, actions, and decisions" (Kramer, 2000, 97). Furthermore, she emphasized the wise person chooses to interact with others in a fashion that encourages openness rather than defensiveness (2000, 86).

Compassion is "an other-oriented emotional state that arises in response to another's suffering and motivates one to act in a prosocial manner to alleviate another's suffering" (Goetz, Keltner and Simon-Thomas 2010, 2). I think, to exercise compassion without getting consumed by the issues and problems of others, a healthy degree of self-compassion is essential.

Self-compassion involves treating yourself with care and concern when considering personal inadequacies, mistakes, failures, and painful life situations (Neff, Kirkpatrick, and Rude 2007). Self-compassion might be a mediating factor in the wise person's behavior. Showing self-compassion, kindness to oneself, might enable the wise person to engage in deeper levels of reflection and self-examination because they avoid critical self-judgment and are patient with themselves. Perhaps self-compassion facilitates the wise person's ability to make sense of and learn from their life experiences more than other people do.

Altruistic behavior is defined as "voluntary behavior intended to benefit another, which is not performed with the expectation of receiving external rewards or avoiding externally produced aversive stimuli or punishments" (Eisenberg and Miller 1987, 92). Typically, altruistic behavior is regarded as a prosocial behavior motivated by a desire to help another or others without benefit to self.

Proponents of altruism claim the underlying motives for much of what we do, including what we do for others, stem from selfish ambition. Yet, they assert at least some of us, to some extent, under certain circumstances, are capable of a qualitatively different form of intention: motivation with an end goal of benefiting someone else (Batson, Ahmad, Lishner, and Tsang 2002, 485-494).

Perhaps the story that follows provides a good example of altruism.

On June 23, 2018, a news story broke in northern Thailand and quickly seized global attention when twelve boys from the Wild Boar junior soccer club and their assistant coach went missing after a practice session. The boys were aged between eleven and sixteen; their coach, twenty-five. Their bicycles were found at the entrance to the Tham Luang Nang Non cave system, which the boys often visited to explore (Peplow 2021).

The monsoon in Northern Thailand usually comes in mid-July, when the caves would become rivers and be closed, but there had been an early storm that day flooding all the cave exits, and more storms were forecast. The boys and their coach were either trapped or had drowned.

Thai Navy SEALs were immediately mobilized, the US deployed military personnel from Japan, and many volunteers rushed to the scene, but it quickly became apparent to the Thai and US divers the diving conditions were way beyond their competence. Fortunately, Vernon Unsworth, a British financial adviser and cave explorer, was on hand. He had spent years exploring the cave system and convinced the Thai minister of the Interior that specialist cave divers were needed. Cave divers are a rare breed. Cave diving is a hobby, not a profession, but Unsworth knew Rick Stanton and John Volanthen, two of the best in the world. On day four of the crisis, Stanton and Volanthen were contacted and flew out from the UK.

On day five, the Thai Navy reluctantly gave Stanton and Volanthen permission to dive the caves. On day six, Stanton and Volanthen discovered and rescued four Thai workers who had become trapped in the caves by rising water. No one had realized they were missing. They continued exploring and laying guidelines deeper into the caves, but despondency had set in, with the US military declaring the search a lost cause.

On July 2, day ten of the search, Stanton and Volanthen entered a chamber 2.5 miles from the cave entrance where they found and filmed what they'd been looking for: the boys and their coach, hungry but alive. The footage was beamed across the world. The Thai Navy announced they'd take over, Stanton and Volanthen were thanked and told their role would now be advisory only, but the Thai divers found the dive beyond their competence, one died, and they ceased their dive efforts.

With the onset of the monsoon now just days away, which would make diving impossible, oxygen levels in the boys' cave dropping dangerously low, and no practical ideas of how to rescue them, Stanton reached out to Richard Harris, an Australian doctor, anesthesiologist, and cave diver, to ask if the boys could be sedated and dived out. Harris said it couldn't be done but set out to Thailand to see how he could help. He quickly realized there was no alternative to save the boys. Stanton and Volanthen called in other expert cave divers to assist, and detailed rescue plans were developed with the Thai and American military.

On day sixteen, with permission finally given by the Thai authorities, Stanton, Volanthen, and their team successfully dived out four boys. On day seventeen four more were rescued, but there were heavy rains that night, making diving conditions even more difficult. On day eighteen, the remaining five were brought out. Nearly ten thousand people had been involved in the rescue efforts and, miraculously, all twelve boys and their coach had been saved (Peplow 2021).

What drives people like Stanton, Volanthen, Harris, and their colleagues to risk their own lives to save others, when the Royal Thai Navy SEALs and US Special Forces did not think the mission was at all possible? Once they had seen the boys and coach, and the reality of their plight, they seemed compelled to act, even when all others could, or would, not.

Elizabeth Chai Vasarhelyi, codirector of *The Rescue*, a National Geographic documentary of the account, described the rescue mission as "a story of great decency and great moral courage, a story of the risks some people are willing to take to save a life" (Peplow 2021).

If you watch the documentary, and I would encourage you to, you will see that Stanton, Volanthen, Harris, and their colleagues went to great lengths to devise a way to get the boys out and to get permission to attempt the rescue. I don't know if they are wise. I cannot say they merged their own interests with the interests of others. But I do think their behavior and actions met all the criteria proposed by Eisenberg and Miller for altruistic behavior.

This chapter took us on a journey from South Africa to Thailand, from the selfless behavior of Nelson Mandela to the epic rescue of twelve Thai boys and their coach. Mandela's decision to forgive, rather than to seek retribution, changed the political landscape of South Africa and the lives of its people forever. People like me were able to exercise their human right to vote in their country's general elections for the very first time, an act that many take for granted across the civilized world.

I have written about the emotional complexity of wise people; the flexibility they have with regards to the range of emotions they experience and the depth and diversity with which they view their own and others' emotions. I have mentioned the beneficial intertwining of cognition and emotion as a critical contributor to the advanced development of wise people. This reciprocal relationship is particularly pertinent when it comes to the adeptness with which the wise regulate their emotions, especially when faced with complex dilemmas. In such circumstances, most people would simply be overwhelmed or flounder, but not so with wise people. They handle crises and difficult circumstances with equanimity and serenity.

But cognition and emotion are not the full picture. Wise people also have a moral advantage. At the very core of their behavior lie values of universalism, benevolence, and a concern for others. The next chapter gives us a deeper look into how wise people merge their self-interests with the interests of others, and who is more qualified than the American "mother of the civil rights movement" to illustrate this convergence.

CHAPTER FIVE

ENLIGHTENED SELF-INTEREST

"Morality is the reason why humans do unselfish things, even at a cost to themselves, for the benefit of a greater good."
—JOSHUA GREENE, *MORAL TRIBES* (2013, 30)

On Thursday, December 1, 1955, a forty-two-year-old seamstress living in Montgomery, Alabama, took her usual bus home from work. While the bus, like all others in the city, was non-descript, it was an emblem of the endemic racial segregation that was rife throughout the South at the time. When the white section of the bus filled up, the driver asked four black passengers to move further to the back to make room for more whites. Three of the individuals complied—after all, the driver's request was backed by state law. Rosa Louise Parks, the fourth passenger, refused. Little did she know her act of civil disobedience and subsequent arrest would set off a protest that would change history (History Online).

Although her actions were, without doubt, in violation of the laws at the time, were they moral?

"People always say that I didn't give up my seat because I was tired, but that isn't true. I was not tired physically," wrote Parks in her autobiography. "No, the only tired I was, was tired of giving in" (History Online).

In this quote, Parks provides us with insight into her thinking. As a black person, she had had enough of being thought of as having less value as a human being than the white man who wished to occupy the seat. Parks would have been aware the local black community were looking for the right opportunity to protest the segregation laws (History Online). Did Parks' defiance provide fuel to the fire? Even so, she could not have imagined how her defiance would fan the flames for the civil rights movement in the United States.

Her actions set in motion the Montgomery Bus Boycott, which was led by a twenty-six-year-old pastor, Martin Luther King, Jr., who consequently became known as a national leader in the struggle for civil rights. The boycott lasted more than a year, during which Parks lost her job, was repeatedly harassed and threatened, and was forced to leave Montgomery. On November 13, 1956, the Supreme Court ruled that bus segregation was unconstitutional. The boycott ended December 20, a day after the Court's written order arrived in Montgomery. Parks became known as "the mother of the civil rights movement" and a nationally recognized symbol of dignity and strength in the struggle to end entrenched racial segregation (History Online).

In 1999, Parks was awarded the Congressional Gold Medal, the highest honor the United States bestows on a civilian. When Rosa Parks died at the age of ninety-two on October 24, 2005, she became the first woman in the nation's history to lie in honor at the US Capitol (History Online).

WHAT DOES IT MEAN TO BE "MORAL"?

The meaning of "morality" and what is "right" and "wrong" causes a good deal of debate and controversy. William Damon, who wrote *The Moral Advantage*, was asked what he meant by the words "moral" and "morality." He answered: "I am simply referring to the morality shared by people of goodwill everywhere. This includes aspirations to make the world a better place, to act decently, to care for one's family and one's neighbors, to live honorably, and to be kind, fair, honest, and responsible" (2004, xii).

Morality, I think, has two parts. The first is foundational and comprises a set of rules about things we should not do, such as cheat, lie, steal, kill, and so on. The second, into which I think we grow with age and experience, is things we ought to do, like doing good, helping others, a sense of service and commitment to a larger purpose and greater good.

During the civil rights movement, many individuals committed acts that at the time were considered criminal but were designed to further the cause of racial equality. History has shown us that Parks' actions were morally justified, even though they were, then, illegal (Robinson 2013).

In time, laws were enacted to end discrimination and to emancipate all those previously disadvantaged, although this journey may not yet be fully completed. Her story reveals that morality and wisdom are inextricably interwoven. What might have seemed like a simple act of defiance had long-range consequences that impacted more than just a few people and on multiple levels.

We find further evidence supporting the consensus that Rosa Parks was an upstanding moral citizen in a study conducted by psychologist Jeremy A. Frimer and his colleagues (Frimer, Walker, Lee, Riches, and Dunlop 2012). They identified examples of those who exemplified moral excellence and others who did not. Parks appeared at the top of the list as exhibiting all five criteria as originally suggested by developmental psychologists Anne Colby and William Damon, who studied contemporary moral exemplars for their book, *Some Do Care* (1992, 29). The five criteria are:

1. "Principled/virtuous: a sustained commitment to moral ideals or principles that include a generalized respect for humanity; or a sustained evidence of moral virtue
2. Consistent: a disposition to act in accord with one's moral ideals or principles, implying also a consistency between one's actions and intentions and between the means and the ends of one's actions
3. Brave: a willingness to risk one's self-interest for the sake of one's moral values
4. Inspiring: a tendency to be inspiring to others and thereby to move them to moral action

5. Humble: a sense of realistic humility about one's own importance relative to the world at large, implying a relative lack of concern for one's own ego."

Those identified as displaying the characteristics of moral excellence included Rosa Parks, Nelson Mandela, Mohandas Gandhi, and Martin Luther King, Jr. (Frimer et. al. 2012, 1127). Those who did not included Adolf Hitler, George W. Bush, Donald Rumsfeld, Vladimir Putin, and Kim Jong II (Frimer et. al. 2012, 1129).

ENLIGHTENED SELF-INTEREST: MORALITY AND WISDOM

The pivotal difference between those who displayed moral excellence and those who did not is that the former exhibited "enlightened self-interest." They see their interests as congruent with those of others and advanced them by promoting the interests of others. Those who did not display moral excellence had not achieved this congruence, advancing, and pursuing their own interests over others' (Frimer et. al. 2012, 1120).

Parks put herself at risk and took a stand against a system that placed her and her fellow black citizens in a lesser position because she had had enough. Her defiance was for herself and her community. At the heart of her actions is "enlightened self-interest" (Frimer, Walker, Dunlop, Lee, and Riches 2011).

We know from psychologist Robert Sternberg's work on wisdom (Sternberg 1986; 1998) that one can be intelligent without being wise, but it is unlikely for a wise person to lack intelligence. I think the same principle applies to morality. You can be a moral exemplar without being wise, but it is unlikely for a wise person to lack moral excellence. Unsurprisingly, many of the individuals Frimer identified as moral exemplars are cited as wisdom exemplars by wisdom researchers Nic M. Weststrate, Michel Ferrari, and Monika Ardelt (2016).

Frimer and his colleagues suggested that for most people the pursuit of their own interests (agency) is psychologically separate from their desire to help others (communion) reach their goals. Either agency or communion is active during any given time. It is rare for both to be active simultaneously. This was not the case for those with moral excellence, prompting the researchers to ask: "How can one advance one's own situation and the plight of others simultaneously? How do moral exemplars integrate these dialectical themes?" (Frimer et. al. 2011, 161). Colby and Damon's analysis of moral exemplars observed, "The exemplars' moral identities become tightly integrated, almost fused, with their self-identities" (1992, 304). When one integrates agency and communion, "agency breathes life into communion, and communion gives agency a greater purpose" (Frimer and Walker 2009, 1677).

Those who research adult moral development suggest it is the discovery, recognition, and acceptance of contradictory emotions, thoughts, and beliefs that propel the adult toward mature moral reasoning (Gilligan and Murphy 1979). One of the defining characteristics of wise individuals seems to be the capacity to balance positive and negative emotions when interpreting contradictions, ambiguities, and uncertainties, as discussed in the preceding chapter.

An individual's moral development, as with affect and cognition, is a journey, an evolution. Glück and Sternberg (2022, 119) observed those at the highest levels of moral development do not view rules as absolute. They recognize that people's needs and values differ, that some rules and values are higher in priority than others, and that rules can be in conflict and must be considered and balanced each against the other. Pasupathi and Staudinger (2001) found those at the highest levels of moral development are likely also to be wise (Glück and Sternberg 2022, 120).

Wise people think deeply about complex issues, are said to care about the greater good, have concern for the well-being of others, and open their thinking to accommodate the opinions of others. They do not particularly care about their personal security and are not at all interested in power and authority (Glück, Gussnig, and Schrottenbacher 2019, 19).

Linda Klebe Treviño and colleagues (2003, 34), who studied the ethical behavior of executives, found that self-centered leaders lacked ethical awareness and cared mainly about themselves and the bottom line, whereas ethical leaders were people focused. They cared about people, respected them, and developed them. The challenge for leaders, it seems, is one of achieving an appropriate balance between the interests of others and self. Is this not "enlightened self-interest"?

Failure to deal appropriately with what seem to be minor moral dilemmas can lead to unexpected and serious outcomes. In summer 2022, France was facing its worst drought since records began in 1959. Water restrictions were introduced across ninety-three of France's ninety-six departments, with water bans imposed on farmers, businesses, and individuals, but, curiously, golf courses had a preexisting exemption that allowed them to continue to water their greens and their tees (Gill 2022).

There are about 730 golf courses in France, and estimated to be 400 to 800,000 golfers, some 0.6 to 1.2 percent of the population. Farmers predicted crop yields to be adversely affected by up to 35 percent, which would force prices up, fueling inflation. Affected businesses' productivity declined. More than one hundred towns were left without piped drinking water, with supplies trucked in (Gill 2022). The country became a tinderbox, with significant forest fires and residents forced to flee their homes. But still, the golf course exemption was not overturned. The Golfing Federation argued, "A golf course without a green is like an ice rink without ice," but who in their right mind would be out playing golf in temperatures well above forty degrees Celsius, or 104 degrees Fahrenheit?

The failure to act in this case led to protestations across the country from farmers, business, and public alike. They were seriously disaffected from government policy, far from aligned in national adversity. Extinction Rebellion (an environmental protest group) characterized the position as "economic madness takes precedence over ecological reason" and took action: they filled the holes on the golf course greens with concrete (Herman 2022).

The values of those in policy and law-making positions were brought seriously into question, as were their abilities to decide where priorities should be allocated and, ultimately, their economic allegiances.

Those things we prioritize in life are the things to which we attach value. Each of us holds values with varying degrees of importance. In my work as an executive coach, I sometimes ask clients to do an exercise around their values. To my delight, one of my clients addressed the subject with me. He had clearly thought about it a great deal, and it was of utmost importance to him. He had placed his family at the top of his "values pyramid" and shared with me how much they meant to him. This was extremely positive to hear because oftentimes leaders think that to place their families above their work would be wrong or inappropriate. I disagree.

MORALITY AND VALUES

I believe one's behavior flows from what one values. I think wise people have very clear views on what they value. This impacts how they view themselves and, consequently, how they view others. Character is closely tied to values. This is particularly revealing when someone is under tremendous pressure. For example, the way they respond usually reveals who or what they care about deeply.

Shalom H. Schwartz, professor emeritus of psychology at the Hebrew University of Jerusalem, identified ten distinct types of universal values recognized across all cultures. They are: power, achievement, hedonism, stimulation, self-direction, universalism, benevolence, tradition, conformity, and security. Some of the values are motivated by self-enhancement, such as power and achievement, because they advance the self. Others are self-transcendent values, such as benevolence and universalism, because they promote the interests of others (Schwartz 2012, 8).

The value orientations of wise individuals are focused on a greater good that extends much further than just members of their immediate circle, to humanity and the world at large. Because they have the breadth and depth to consider many perspectives when thinking about moral issues and dealing with the emotional and social aspects of complex situations, they are better able and more likely to also act ethically when faced with challenging situations (Sternberg and Glück 2022, 130).

At the end of the day, regardless of what values you espouse, it all comes down to Norma Haan's eloquent statement: "Action (*rather than just thought*) is nearer to being the litmus test for bona fide morality" (Haan, Aerts, and Cooper 1985, 53—Italics added). The action we take, the way we behave, is what determines whether we are morally wise.

Earlier in this chapter, we saw how Rosa Parks' actions were considered criminal, but only when judged against laws that were subsequently deemed to be morally flawed.

Wisdom does not always conform to the acknowledged standard of right or wrong but pushes the boundaries to define anew what should be acceptable, morally justifiable, and universal. Sometimes, laws need to be challenged and changed for the better.

What follows is a story of a man wrongfully accused, his child being placed in foster care, and, eventually, a law being introduced that saves others from the same fate.

Christopher Ratte, a professor at the University of Michigan, Ann Arbor, took his seven-year-old son, Leo, to a Detroit Tigers game on April 4, 2008. He stopped at a Comerica Park concession stand to buy the thirsty boy some lemonade, completely unaware of its alcohol content. It wasn't until the top of the ninth inning when a security guard questioned Ratte about the bottle in his son's hand that Ratte learned of the drink's alcohol content. When he tried to look at the bottle, the security guard snatched it. Police responded. The boy was examined by Comerica Park medical staff, who found no problems. Yet Leo was taken by ambulance to Detroit's Children's Hospital because clinic officials said the boy reported feeling a little nauseated. A blood sample taken at the hospital detected no trace of alcohol. He was cleared to go home but instead was taken by the County Children's Protective Services (CPS), a division of the state Department of Human Services (Agar 2011).

At the time of this incident, Michigan law permitted the emergency removal of children if there was even the slightest hint of danger to their health, morals, or welfare (Agar 2011).

CPS would not allow Leo to go home with his mother, Claire, who was not at the game. "The first night, Leo slept on a couch in the CPS building with his parents waiting outside on the sidewalk. The next day, he was sent to a foster home," the American Civil Liberties Union (ACLU) of Michigan told reporters. He was released to his mother after three days, but his father had to move out of the house until the case was eventually dropped three days later (Agar 2011).

Claire Ratte, also a professor at the University of Michigan, said, "If the University of Michigan had not helped us, it could have taken weeks to get Leo back. It's tremendously important for us to challenge this law so that no other family has to deal with the lasting effects of having a child unjustly removed" (Agar 2011).

Ratte and his wife filed a formal complaint with the Child Protective Services ombudsman. The goal of their lawsuit was to change Michigan law so that only children who are at substantial risk of harm or in surroundings that present an imminent risk of harm are taken away from their parents. Four years after Christopher and Claire began their legal battle, "Leo's Law" was finally passed (Agar 2011).

We cannot always control what happens in our lives, and wise people are better at understanding this than most of us. We can, however, manage how we respond to the events that befall us.

On that day in April when Ratte's son was taken away from him, he probably wished he had never set foot at that ballgame with Leo. But these events, however awful, have led to the law being rewritten to protect, rather than violate, human rights. Christopher and Claire responded not only by successfully getting their son back from foster care, but they went further. They fought to overturn the law so that other people who are wrongly accused don't have to suffer what they did.

It might appear that Christopher and Claire are simply reacting to a sequence of events in which they were wronged. But why would they spend four years of their busy lives and their finances protesting a law that might not affect them again? Claire was emphatic they did not want other families to have to endure a child being unjustly removed from parents. This demonstrated values of benevolence and universalism, values that showed a concern for others.

Aristotle might well interpret their actions as practical wisdom. Aristotle saw practical wisdom as the crucial capacity human beings need for making good choices—a form of wisdom in action (Schwartz and Sharpe 2019, 227).

John Kekes, professor emeritus of philosophy at the University at Albany, New York State, said: "To understand wisdom, we have to understand its connection with knowledge, action, and judgment" (1980, 277). In this chapter, we have encountered a few stories which explore this. At the outset of the chapter, Rosa Parks, an ordinary woman, boarded a bus, and by the time she got off her actions had set in motion a sequence of events that changed history. Parks' actions, which were illegal at the time, led her to be described as a moral exemplar. We saw how moral exemplars exhibit "enlightened self-interest." They advance their own interests while promoting the interests of others, a behavior associated with wisdom. The values of moral exemplars are undoubtedly tilted toward other-directedness and benevolence. Parks may not be considered wise, but her actions certainly benefited many black people in America.

When William Damon was asked what he meant by the words "moral" and "morality," his answer was something each of us could aspire to practice: "To make the world a better place... to be kind, fair, honest, and responsible" (2004, xii). We don't have to be moral exemplars, but each of us can practice ethical, other-centered behaviors that align with our values.

CHAPTER SIX

TRANSCENDING THE SELF

"Between stimulus and response there is a space. In that space is our power to choose our response. In our response lies our growth and our freedom."

—VIKTOR FRANKL, *MAN'S SEARCH FOR MEANING*

The story of Job, originally from the Christian and Judaic traditions, is about a man who became the object of a challenge between God and Satan. Job suffered great devastation, but his response to the catalogue of disasters was atypical.

Job was extremely wealthy, greatly respected, and admired. He had a large family, seven sons and three daughters. He owned extensive flocks of livestock and a very great household, so much so that he was the greatest of all the men of the East. Satan challenged God saying that Job was only a good man because he had everything he could want in his life. God met Satan's challenge and allowed him to test Job (Book of Job, NIV).

In the space of a few days, Job lost almost all his material possessions, all ten children, his servants, and his entire body broke out in painful weeping sores. His wife rejected him, and his trusted friends thought he may have brought his ordeals upon himself. Alone, rejected, and misunderstood, Job eventually responded to these losses with remarkable equanimity. Refusing to engage in self-pity, "Job struggles for some truer, transcendent meaning of self" (Achenbaum and Orwoll 1991, 26).

Job asked God about suffering, particularly his own. Through God's answers, he learned how little control, power, and knowledge he had. Even though he had lost almost everything and everyone, one important thing was not lost: his humility, an essential component of the wise individual's behavior (Achenbaum and Orwoll 1991).

He tore his clothes and shaved his head in mourning (Book of Job), signifying a relinquishing of things as they were, a letting go of his old ways, and to be quiet (he says no more). Although fully aware of his many failings, Job nevertheless stops grieving. "Job demonstrates the complex, dynamic, yet integrative nature of growing wise" (Achenbaum and Orwoll 1991, 23).

Although Job's story is one of immense suffering, he emerges from his pain to teach us a few lessons about wisdom. His story is one of self-transcendence and humility. His trials revealed the lack of control and power he had over the things in his life. I said earlier that Job's response to his ordeal was atypical. Even his trusted friends could not understand it. Later in this chapter, I will discuss another individual, Viktor Frankl, who suffered greatly and, like Job, responded to his torment with hope and a renewed sense of purpose.

Michael R. Levenson, associate professor of human development, Oregon State University, and his colleagues described Job's response in this way: "By accepting his suffering and by seeking deeper understanding of his relationship with God, Job is transformed" (Levenson, Jennings, Aldwin, and Shiraishi 2005, 129). They describe his transformation as self-transcendence. Job accepted who he is, including his weaknesses, abandoned his need for external validation, and developed a greater focus on others. For these authors, self-transcendence is equivalent to wisdom and implies "the dissolution of (self-based) obstacles to empathy, understanding, and integrity" (2005, 129).

Job took counsel from respected friends to gain perspective on his behaviors and past actions. He reflected deeply, searched his own motives, and scrutinized the morality of his thoughts and deeds. This mature form of introspective awareness, a vulnerability to embrace the unknown and an openness to experience, reveals an ability to both respond wisely and grow in wisdom through the ordeals he suffered (Achenbaum and Orwoll 1991).

In response, God doubled Job's fortune, gave him a new family of seven sons and three daughters, and allowed him to live another one hundred and forty years (Book of Job, NIV). His life was enriched because of the way he chose to deal with his torment.

In chapter three, we saw how the decisions of wise people can push standards to new limits that redefine the acceptable. Job's final act did exactly this: he defied convention by leaving his daughters an inheritance equal to that of their brothers, a practice unheard of at that time (circa fifth century BCE; Britannica).

The story of Job is an extreme one—not the kind of ordeal you and I would want to endure. However, Job's account has much to teach us about growing in wisdom. We do not need to suffer Job's ordeals to learn important life lessons. We can see from his story that if we reflect upon life's challenges and our faults, failings, and fears and learn to embrace and navigate them, we too may gain some wisdom.

Job's story has many lessons that illuminate the journey to becoming wise. They are not, however, by any means the only factors that can contribute toward this journey.

REFLECTING ON LIFE EXPERIENCES

To reflect is to think deeply and carefully about something. To self-reflect is to evaluate, meditate upon, and think deeply and carefully about one's attitudes, values, and beliefs; one's thoughts, actions, and behaviors.

Self-reflection is a process that enhances one's ability to make sense of life experiences. Depending on the experience one reflects upon, this process might be emotionally negative and arduous, leading some to engage in a lesser version of it, whilst others refrain entirely. The kind of self-reflection beneficial to developing wisdom, however, must be of a certain quality and depth (Weststrate 2019, 502).

Researchers have identified two forms of reflection: redemptive reflection and exploratory reflection. The former involves "positively reframing and moving on from the event emotionally" and does not necessarily lead to wisdom. The latter requires "going deeper into the meaning of the event" (Weststrate and Glück 2017, 6).

When someone engages in redemptive reflection, they tell the story of an experience in a way that makes them feel good. They do not delve deeper into the experience, as this act might elicit negative emotions or may just be too painful. Redemptive reflection provides the individual with an acceptance of what has happened, of closure, and the regaining of some form of happiness and sense of normality (Webster, Weststrate, Ferrari, Munroe, and Pierce 2018; Weststrate and Glück 2017).

A person engaging in exploratory reflection considers the deeper meaning of the whole experience, a process that can promote personal growth. The regular practice of exploratory reflection can enable deeper levels of self-insight, self-knowledge, and self-awareness, which form the basis of wise behavior. It is this iterative process of constant reflection, and modifying of perspectives and behaviors, that helps wise people abandon those defense mechanisms that inhibit transformation, to make sense of life experiences, and to grow from and through them. Wise individuals were found to practice exploratory reflection (Weststrate and Glück 2017).

Wisdom is acquired over time by making sense of one's life experiences, particularly the most challenging ones, often through painful confrontation with one's own inadequacies. Wise people reflect on their own life experiences, and those of others, to make sense of and to deepen their understanding of themselves. Intense introspection, a willingness to challenge conventional ideas, and the flexibility to change one's views based on new information are essential features of wisdom (Achenbaum and Orwoll 1991).

Wise people are deeply self-aware. Their flaws and mistakes do not diminish them. Rather, they see them as opportunities for self-growth. They are constantly trying to understand the origins or root causes to address and to integrate them. Wise people spend a great deal of time and effort enhancing their levels of objectivity, a process that requires understanding, accepting, and addressing their fears and weaker areas. As discussed in chapter four, they practice self-compassion, which might enable them to engage in deeper levels of reflection and self-examination because they avoid critical self-judgment and are patient with themselves.

As individuals develop in wisdom, they are increasingly likely to engage in deeper and more analytical forms of self-reflection. Across their adult life, wise people modify the way they go about reflecting and making sense of their experiences. They constantly learn to identify their own defense mechanisms, biases, and blind spots, which would otherwise prevent them from engaging in still deeper levels of critical self-examination (Weststrate and Glück 2017).

QUIETING THE EGO

We have all met people we consider to be egotistical, full of themselves, and arrogant. As I write this, a particular "gentleman" I met several years ago comes to mind. The whole of our conversation—or should I say, his monologue—was about how wonderful and accomplished he was. He was supposed to be talking about his team and why he thought my services might be of use to help them work together more effectively. But all he was interested in was boasting about his own importance. This man had a noisy ego, only interested in his own needs, his own status, and how these can be satisfied. His behavior was self-aggrandizing. This is far removed from the behavior of someone who has a quiet ego, or from that of wise individuals.

In 2005, psychologists Heidi Wayment and Jack Bauer coined the term "quiet ego." It focuses on balancing the interests of self and others and cultivating growth of the self and of others over time. A quiet ego does not mean a lesser or silenced ego. It is not low confidence, not low self-esteem, nor is it a disregard for one's immediate self-interest. A person with a quiet ego acknowledges their own limitations, is comfortable in their own skin, doesn't need to resort to defensiveness whenever the ego is challenged or threatened, and has a secure sense of self-worth and competence (Wayment and Bauer 2018).

The quiet ego transcends self-focused, self-centered behavior, not by neglecting the self but rather by balancing concern for self with concern for others. This enables the growth and development of the self and others over time. When one's ego is quiet, one is motivated and able to consider others' perspectives, empathize with others who are different to oneself, view situations and issues non-defensively, and see each situation as an opportunity for growth and for prosocial development. A quieter ego is compassionate and emotionally regulated. Someone with a quiet ego is highly likely to practice self-compassion, so unlikely to judge themselves and, possibly, others critically. Wayment and Bauer found that the quiet ego and self-compassion are important resources for finding meaning in the context of a life event that is often threatening (Wayment and Bauer 2017, 87).

A quiet ego helps us be receptive to perspectives that are very different to ours, enabling us to stay open to new information. Wayment and Bauer believe a focus on one's important values may help an individual reduce one's sense of threat and defensiveness (2018, 12). They found that a quiet ego was strongly related to Schwartz's self-transcendence values of universalism, benevolence, and self-direction (independent thought and action—choosing, creating, exploring), as discussed in chapter five (Wayment and Bauer 2017, 9). Also, Glück and Sternberg (2022, 126) reported that several studies found the values most important to wise people are universalism, benevolence, and self-direction.

A quietened (or quieted) ego is achieved when the individual grows beyond the fear of attacks upon, and the need to protect the self, to a self-transcendent focus. A secure sense of self, a relatively low self-focus where there is no longer the need or desire to feed the ego, is a prerequisite for humility.

HUMILITY

"Humility is not thinking less of yourself, it's thinking of yourself less."

—C.S. LEWIS

True humility is a sign the person has accepted themselves for who they truly are, accepting both strengths and weaknesses; a realization that no one is perfect and that we continue to evolve, to grow, to improve. Humble people are capable of assessing their own behavior honestly. Humility should not be mistaken for a sense of inferiority or weakness, but rather a lack of self-aggrandizing biases (Kesibir 2014, 611).

June Price Tangney, professor of psychology at George Mason University, Fairfax, Virginia, writes, "Humility carries with it an open-mindedness, a willingness to admit mistakes and seek advice, and a desire to learn" (2002, 412). Some of Tangney's descriptions of humility are very similar to those of wise behavior.

In chapter five, I considered the research by Frimer and colleagues, who used the five criteria proposed by Colby and Damon to characterize moral excellence, to assess a number of people said to be moral exemplars. To qualify as a moral exemplar, the candidates had to display all five criteria. One of those criteria was "humble: a sense of realistic humility about one's own importance relative to the world at large, implying a relative lack of concern for one's own ego" (1992, 29). So, it would seem that humility is a key component of both morality and wisdom.

The opposite of humility is pride. Proud people will rarely admit they don't know something or have the answer to a question. They can exhibit a marked reluctance to accept new information, particularly if it doesn't fit with their worldview, and do not respond well to what they perceive as criticism. I have often found this to be a facade to cover a deep-seated insecurity and, in some instances, low self-esteem, and can be accompanied by arrogance and aggression. Don't be put off by their behavior. They need your compassion and your understanding.

Remember the "gentleman" I referred to earlier with the noisy ego? I found him to be quite fragile. He was incapable of receiving feedback he perceived as negative. He described such feedback as judgmental and useless. Paradoxically, he proved to be decidedly judgmental.

If a quieting of the ego toward self-transcendence is required to attain the highest levels of psychological development, and an accurate perception and an acceptance of reality is a prerequisite to wisdom, then it would seem humility is an essential component of psychological maturity and of wisdom.

SELF-TRANSCENDENCE

"Self-transcendence involves a fundamental shift in one's life attitude, from an egotistic focus to caring for others or something greater than oneself" (Wong, Mayer, and Bowers 2020, 1).

Self-transcendence describes a tendency to move through and beyond self-focused issues to more other-directed, universal concerns. A robust sense of self and self-acceptance is necessary before one can focus on issues beyond self. Orwoll and Perlmutter (1990) viewed self-transcendence as an essential component of wisdom. They believed it accounts in part for wise people's long-range perspectives and deep understanding of complex issues.

Clinical psychologist Deirdre Kramer observed that wise people "seem able to first embrace and then transcend self-concerns to integrate their capacity for introspection with a deep and abiding concern for human relationships and generative concern for others" (2000, 100).

Self-transcendence is built upon a strong sense of self, a healthy self-esteem and self-worth. With this secure basis in place, one can abandon self-focus and selfish ambition, and replace them with other-focus and service to others.

Viktor Frankl, psychotherapist and Holocaust survivor, was a strong proponent of self-transcendence. He believed that to be fully human and to flourish, we must make sense of our existence in the world and that our existence is not authentic unless it involves the self-transcendent quality of this form of attention, beyond us and toward meaning. It is in the act of finding meaning that we take responsibility for our own lives. He recommended three possible ways we can find meaning in our lives:

1. In the creation of work, deeds, or actions;
2. Through the experience of something or someone; and
3. By the attitude we choose to adopt when we face unavoidable suffering.

"To speak about the meaning and value of life may seem more necessary today than ever." In 1946, Frankl opened one of a series of talks in Vienna with these words. His talk was about what his experience of incarceration in Nazi death camps had taught him about the human condition. The previous year, Frankl had been a prisoner in Auschwitz, a concentration camp where more than a million people were killed in the gas chambers (Malik 2020). He spent three years in four concentration camps. Both his parents, his brother, and his first wife died in the camps.

Viktor Emil Frankl was born on March 26, 1905, in Vienna, Austria. He was a psychiatrist and psychotherapist who developed the psychological approach known as logo-therapy (Greek for "healing through meaning"). Frankl believed the primary motivation of an individual is the search for meaning in life, and the primary purpose of psychotherapy should be to help the individual find that meaning (Viktor Frankl Institute, n.d.). Such is the signif-icance of his work that it is widely recognized as the third school of Viennese psychotherapy (the first was Sigmund

Freud, the second Alfred Adler). Vienna was home to all three, and their theories provided the foundations to much of how the western world views psychotherapy today. Frankl died in 1997 at age ninety-two.

Frankl was so interested in psychology that he began taking adult night classes when he was in junior high school. As a teenager, he corresponded with Freud and then joined Adler's school for a time. He studied philosophy and learned hypnosis at the age of fifteen. Frankl published his first scholarly article when he was eighteen, and by twenty-two he was lecturing on the meaning of life (Viktor Frankl Institute, n.d.).

He worked as a psychiatrist, not only to help his patients but also to learn from them. He did so up to the point of his captivity in 1942. During the time he was held in the concentration camps, he observed the brutality and degradation around him and theorized that those inmates who had some purpose in their lives were more likely to survive. He, himself, tried to recreate the manuscript of a book he had been writing before his capture (Viktor Frankl Institute, n.d.).

Following liberation, Frankl returned to Vienna, where he found nothing left of the life he once knew and the people he loved. He focused on reconstructing his manuscript on logotherapy, which had been taken from him at the first camp. The English translation of Frankl's *Man's Search for Meaning* was published in 1959 and became an international bestseller. He saw this success not so much as a personal achievement but as a symptom of the mass neurosis of modern times, since its title promised to deal with the question of life's meaningfulness (Viktor Frankl Institute, n.d.).

When I first went to university, I knew I wanted to use my studies to help others. My first job after my bachelor's degree showed me I should help in a corporate, rather than clinical, setting. After my master's and whilst working for Warner Burke in New York, I had the enormous privilege to work with C-suite leaders from Fortune 500 companies on their development. Here, I realized two critical things: First, any positive changes in their behavior we were able to bring about affected not just the leaders but also those who worked around them and, potentially, the whole company. The effects of our interventions were multiplied. The second was that to be as effective as my work colleagues in helping such leaders, I would need to become better versed in my subject matter, and that would require me to study for a PhD at some point.

In 1998, I returned to Cape Town, South Africa, and took up the role of head of corporate learning with Shell South Africa. Unfortunately, the role turned out to be pretty frustrating, largely because most of the leadership team were not greatly motivated to pursue their personal development. Development was something they thought their staff needed but saw little benefit for themselves. I provided help where I could, and we made some gains. But they would have been far greater if the leadership had been more involved. During this time, I gained heart from reading some of Frankl's work and decided it was time for my PhD.

The PhD led me to "levels of psychological development," particularly in leaders and leadership, and equipped me with tools I use today with my clients to help them develop. I've come to see I seriously underestimated the impacts of any positive changes in their behavior we achieve. The impacts extend well beyond the leader's corporate setting. They are carried into homes, are relayed into communities, and can be passed on to their children. I now recognize that I, too, am changed as I help others. Hopefully, we are all being nudged along our journeys to greater wisdom.

When I reflect upon where I have come from and where I am now, I realize how immensely fortunate I have been. Some of this has come from hard work but still more has come from the people along the way who saw something in me and have provided guidance and encouragement. I realize I have had many opportunities that others have not, and for these I am truly grateful. And so, from day to day, I try to pay back all that good fortune by helping others as best I can.

"Life is never made unbearable by circumstances, but only by lack of meaning and purpose."
—VIKTOR FRANKL, *MAN'S SEARCH FOR MEANING*

Frankl's philosophy has been greatly influential across the world. Paul Wong, psychologist, researcher, and speaker, has formulated a model of self-transcendence based on Frankl's work. Wong's ideas are based on understanding your own identity and purpose before you can be of "wise" service to others. He suggested that the more we "forget ourselves in the act of giving ourselves to a cause, service, or love, the more human we become and, in turn, realize who we truly are" (Worth and Smith 2021, 3). He views self-transcendence as a journey or process in which we are continuously improving to expand our potential. This journey is not in service of self but in service to others.

Wong suggested three steps to stimulate the development of self-transcendence (Worth and Smith 2021, 3–4):
1. Seeking meaning through pursuing one's values, some form of mindfulness meditation, and maintaining an attitude of openness, curiosity, and compassion;
2. Seeking a calling that goes way beyond one's work or career to find an expression of who one really is, one's unique talents, linking to a higher purpose or serving a greater good; and
3. Seeking ultimate meaning beyond one's current context, physical limitations, time, and space to a transcendental realm. This might involve a spiritual experience for some or notions of goodness, truth, and beauty for others. This level of transcendence reflects deeply held beliefs, values, and worldviews.

The primary goal of this chapter has been to explain how reflection can be a route to wisdom and how wise people use the process of reflection to deepen their self-understanding and self-knowledge—and their knowledge and understanding of others. Viktor Frankl's message of meaning and purpose provides a great lesson: We should each try to find something to pursue that is important and has deep meaning to us. However, wisdom is so much more than pursuing meaning and purpose in one's life. It involves transcending the self; cultivating a quiet ego to provide the space to recognize areas for growth in oneself; developing the ability to see the essence of people and problems with unbiased clarity; and providing advice, guidance, and solutions that are apposite, penetrating, and may well be novel.

PART III

BECOMING WISE

CHAPTER SEVEN

GROWING IN WISDOM

For many years, Grace kept a terrible secret from almost everyone in her life: a childhood fraught with a consistent barrage of psychological trauma from both parents and sexual abuse at the hands of her father.

Many might crumble under the constant attack on self-worth, but Grace would, in time, find a way to turn all this adversity into her greatest asset.

Grace was the youngest of three children. Her sister was six years older than her, and her brother was eighteen months older. Her sister endured years of sexual abuse from their father, and her brother suffered regular severe beatings. When Grace's sister told their mother about the sexual abuse, both girls were made to feel as though they were encouraging their father's abominable behavior.

Grace said, "My mother told me I was not allowed to sit on the sofa with my legs up. She told me to put my legs down and make sure my skirt was pulled down. As I grew older and began to develop breasts my mum took me to get some bras. I was told not to draw attention to the fact I was maturing."

Grace endured a catalogue of abuse growing up. Both parents constantly compared Grace to her older siblings in a way that made her feel worthless. She was repeatedly told how good her sister was at math and how good her brother was at school, and that she was not good at anything. This abuse resulted in her always feeling insecure, unloved, and stupid. To top it all, the family nicknamed her "Stupid."

She told me, "I just didn't feel I was worth anything, I suppose. It took me a long while to get over all the other things, like feeling useless, not accepted, and unloved. And that's what I felt, unloved. It wasn't until I was in my thirties that I was ready to deal with it."

In pursuit of perspective and understanding, Grace read books on abuse. She studied the subject. She attended courses, one of which she found so useful she attended multiple times. Then she went for one-to-one counseling. And, above all, she reflected. She says her Christian faith developed along the way. "It became my bedrock. My faith enabled me to forgive my parents, to forgive myself, and to find emotional healing," she told me.

I asked Grace about the time lapse between the abuse and when she dealt with it. She said, "Because I thought it was something that happened to everybody, I just felt powerless. Also, I had tried to bury everything and hope it would go away. It took a very long time to make sense of it all."

Grace emphasized, "The process wasn't just about the abuse. It was more about finding out who I really was. I read so many books and, along with the courses, I began to see I was worthy, I wasn't stupid, and I was loved. It was a long and sometimes painful process, especially when I accepted the fact I could do nothing about the injustice I felt except forgive."

I asked how her past has changed the way she now thinks, feels, and responds to things.

"I'm very protective of people in abusive situations, especially women. Adults and children, irrespective of gender, find it extremely difficult to trust someone enough to tell them what's happening in their lives. I find it very humbling.

"I'm also quite reflective," Grace told me. "People will tell me things, I think about what they've told me, and go back to them later. I find that reflecting on what I have heard helps me to weigh up my responses, rather than say the first thing that comes into my mind."

Grace believes the development of wisdom can start quite young if the child has "gone through some hard experiences." She believes you can grow wiser by having positive life experiences but was quite emphatic that "when you go through tough experiences, there is a greater depth and level of understanding that comes with having been through something tough that maybe is not there were it a positive or just an ordinary experience."

She said, "You can read about these things, have knowledge of them, maybe have some answers. But when you've been through something, there are so many different aspects to it... greater depth and levels of understanding."

> *Resilience research has shown that having a single person, be it a family member, like an aunt or a nursery schoolteacher or whoever, who showed a child love and care early in life, can make all the difference to how they recover from the trauma. One of those circumstantial aspects that I think are as important as a person's inner strengths (Judith Glück personal correspondence 2023).*

More recently, Grace was diagnosed with two different types of cancers. She told me, "It was not quite as bad as my childhood!" She'd long since found her faith and had developed the resilience and wisdom to cope with the diagnoses and see her through "the difficult times."

Grace has turned all the hurt of her dreadful upbringing into something positive. She qualified as a counselor and now uses her powerful, empathic, discerning, and transformative skills to support others. She works as a volunteer counselor at a few charities, drawing on her own life experiences to counsel, mentor, and advise others in need, and is an active member of her local church and involved in several volunteer activities.

Monika Ardelt conducted in-depth interviews in which participants were asked about their religion and spirituality, attitudes toward death and dying, and their most recent positive and negative events. Of the three individuals who scored high on wisdom, she found all three described their religious and spiritual beliefs as having deepened and grown stronger over the years. This process, said Ardelt, "resulted in a decrease in self-centeredness and the development of humility and a quieter ego" (Ardelt 2008, 226; see also chapter six). She also described their attitudes toward life as expressed through a "commitment to serve, a commitment to give, and ethical conduct in their lives" (Ardelt 2008, 229).

Several wisdom researchers consider challenging life experiences as the bedrock for growth in wisdom because such events are often processed at a much deeper level than ordinary or positive incidences (Webster, Weststrate, Ferrari, Munroe, and Pierce 2018). But exposure alone to such events will not lead toward wisdom. Reflection is essential (see chapter six).

Judith Glück (2022, 175), a pioneering researcher of how to develop wisdom, posed this question: "Why (do) some people learn things from life that make them wiser, while other people may go through very similar experiences without gaining any wisdom?"

Grace's story has given us some insight into the answer. Even though it took her many years, she has acknowledged and accepted there was a problem to start with. Others find it extremely difficult to acknowledge they have gone or are going through something challenging. They reframe the experience in a way that restores their sense of well-being and happiness, allows them to move on, and to get back to their "normal." They do not delve deeper into the experience because this, they fear, might be too painful. This reframing might seem like an easy option, but it doesn't lead to freedom, and it is not the path to becoming wise. For that, deeper reflection is required.

One of the most important lessons I learned from Grace's story was that she had to begin her journey of healing by understanding herself, accepting and forgiving herself, and then learning to love herself. With this self-understanding, she was then able to stop allowing others to tell her who and what she was or is.

"No one can make you feel inferior without your consent."
—ELEANOR ROOSEVELT, AMERICAN DIPLOMAT,
HUMANITARIAN, AND FIRST LADY

DEVELOPING INSIGHT

"Applicants for wisdom do what I have done: inquire within."
—HERACLITUS, PHILOSOPHER, 500 BCE

One reason why some people grow in wisdom while others do not seems to be the deep insight they develop into their own behavior. By deep insight I am referring to a profound level of self-knowledge and self-understanding: one's deep feelings, emotions, thoughts, values, assumptions, and so on. Both self-knowledge and self-understanding are constantly evolving within the individual, and as they do, levels of self-awareness continue to grow in tandem. Deep insight is most effectively cultivated through the process of self-reflection and critical self-examination.

Over some twenty-years working as an executive coach, I have noticed time and again those clients who experience the greatest transformations in their lives tend to make the changes in themselves first. As they grew in knowledge and understanding of their own behavior, the subsequent increases in self-awareness allowed for a deeper understanding of others' perspectives, especially when these differed vastly from their own.

A particular client comes to mind, Remy, who was extremely successful at his job but, according to senior colleagues, abrasive with juniors and those whom he considered "lazy" or "incompetent." His company suggested he get my assistance because his behavior was holding him back from further promotions. Remy was extremely keen to meet with me to, as he put it, "get this sorted so I can move on." When I met Remy, he was arrogant, impatient, and didn't care about anyone but himself. Several years later, Remy is a very different person. According to his latest 360-feedback, he now listens patiently to others, is less-judgmental and more accommodating of others' differences, and the real prize was someone described Remy as having become "much more considerate of others."

It was clear from the outset that Remy had very little understanding of how his behavior was perceived by others in his team and in the wider organization. So, it was critical to get some in-depth feedback from his major stakeholders (his 360-feedback). But I had to get the timing right. Providing him with their feedback too early in our process would not be beneficial because Remy would simply dismiss it as "only their opinions." One of my first priorities was to show him how others felt when he was blaming and criticizing them and to understand why, then to look for ways he could be more understanding, explain to team members what his expectations were, show them the standard of work he expected, and take the necessary time to train them.

Remy and I worked together for a period of some two years. Part of Remy's challenge was his inability to view his behavior as part of the problem. He needed to understand he was an active participant, and by changing the way he behaved he would cause the behavior of the team also to change. I was delighted to see the changes in Remy and his behavior as he grew in self-awareness.

Remy, and others like him, may not necessarily grow in wisdom, but armed with greater self-awareness, they are better placed to reflect more realistically and authentically on their life experiences. They can apply the gained insights to themselves but are not yet able to apply them to others, especially those who are different from them. Should they continue along this development path, their capacity to understand and utilize their insights will continue to evolve. As people develop psychologically, more and more of what was previously hidden and unconscious becomes recognizable, and they are then able to address such issues.

Reflection can shift behavior from groupthink and inauthenticity toward individual reasoning, deeper insight, and, in some, wisdom. The wise achieve deep reasoning and greater understanding of implications, meanings, and realities (Walsh 2015).

I asked the people I interviewed for this book to tell me about the wisest person they knew. I asked them where they thought that wisdom had come from or what had happened in their lives that promoted the development of their wisdom. Each wise person identified had a different trajectory. It was clear from the interviewees' answers the development of wisdom is a highly individual process. It follows, however, an evolutionary path from concern with self, to some others, to all others, or as Ken Wilbur, philosopher and writer on transpersonal psychology, put it, from "egocentric, to ethnocentric, to world centric" (Walsh 2015, 287).

LEARNING FROM AND MAKING SENSE OF LIFE EXPERIENCES

"Wisdom comes from experience, but not just any experience will do"

(SCHWARTZ AND SHARPE 2019, 245).

One of the main paths to growing in wisdom is through life experiences. Some believe wisdom comes only from going through traumatic life experiences. Others are of the opinion that transformative experiences don't need to be negative; they can also be positive. Psychologists Judith Glück and Susan Bluck have spent many years researching how people's life experiences contribute or not to cultivating wisdom. They believe the main characteristic of wisdom-fostering experiences is that they transform a person's life or, at least, a person's views about life. However, this is only one part of the life experiences equation. There is another crucial component to it: the person has to take the time to make sense of the experiences.

Grace wanted desperately to understand and to make sense of why her parents treated her so badly. Her faith gave her the courage, she said, to confront these difficult questions in the safety of a counselor who helped her to understand her own position—not to blame her parents, but rather to consider how their own dysfunctional upbringings might have contributed to their treatment of her and to find forgiveness. In Grace's words, "Every time I think I've dealt with a particular hurt or aspect of my past, still another layer appears, much like an onion. I know there will be still more layers that will need to be peeled."

Here, Grace shows us what a powerful catalyst forgiveness is in the healing process. When one is able to understand the background of those who harm others, it can help toward the path of forgiveness, which, in turn, leads to healing. I also noticed that Grace has a great deal of gratitude for the people and things in her life.

Although many researchers have described factors that play a role in how people develop wisdom, they have failed to make clear exactly how individuals learn from their experiences. "Which ways of dealing with and thinking about experiences can help people to grow wiser?" is another pertinent question raised by Glück (2022, 178).

People on the pathway to wisdom are often driven by a deep curiosity about life (Ardelt 2003). They want to understand themselves, their experiences, other people, and the world. It appears it is not just life experience per se that promotes the development of wisdom, it's the types of life experiences, the kinds of challenges one is faced with, and then, of even greater importance, how one responds to these challenges that propels the individual toward wiser thoughts, words, and deeds.

When Grace spoke about her on-going journey of self-discovery and healing, she quite excitedly told me, "I have this hunger and thirst to know things, and I'm always curious to learn new things. I want to know how things work—how the body works, how the mind works, how everything works. I want to delve deeper and deeper into understanding my own behavior so I can be better equipped to help others."

It is the way in which we think about and consider the things that happen to us that can lead us to wise insights. Any experience that challenges a person's views on life has the potential to provoke deeper insight and learning in that it can reveal new experiences, perspectives, and worldviews. These experiences can be positive, negative, or mixed, such as a loving couple having their first child, a tragic divorce or death of a loved one, or moving to another country (Glück 2022, 178).

THE PATH THAT LEADS TO WISDOM

Psychologists Ursula Staudinger and Ute Kunzmann (2005, 321) suggested two "interdependent" paths people are likely to follow in responding to their life challenges. One is the "adjustment pathway": They find ways to adjust their way of living to new circumstances and then continue living their life. The second is the "growth pathway": When they encounter a challenge, they actively try to learn from it. They think deeply about the significance of the experience, what lessons can be learned from it, and then seek to integrate the event into the way they think about life in general.

People who follow the growth pathway are reflecting on their life experiences in a very particular way, which helps them to make sense of their experiences, a crucial ingredient in the recipe to becoming wise. In chapter six, I discussed it's not just any kind of reflection that fosters wise behavior, but the individual's capacity for exploratory reflection (going deeper into the meaning of the event). Weststrate and Glück (2017) found that exploratory reflection was used extensively by wise individuals to help them make sense of life experiences and to grow from and through these. People on a growth pathway are likely to engage in exploratory reflection, which may augment their development of wisdom (Webster et. al. 2018, 131).

As Grace recounted her story and spoke about her life now, it seemed to me she is on the growth pathway. She wants to learn all that she can, not only about her own situation but also about things in general. She has a curious and inquiring mind. She still reads books about self-development to gain further understanding and clarity about her life experiences to make still deeper sense of them. Perhaps humility enables wise people to be open to experience—curious, willing, and receptive to learning new things. Grace certainly abounds with humility.

Wisdom emerges because of the individual's continuous curiosity about people and situations and deep desire for ongoing learning, which is evoked by being open to different points of view and an understanding they don't already have all the answers. They are fully cognizant of the uncertainty and uncontrollability of the future but are unfazed by it because they have developed an increasing faith in their own ability to handle whatever might happen. They try to understand and make sense of their life experiences in a way that provides them with deep insights, lessons learned, and what to do and not do should something similar arise. They share their life lessons openly and generously with others so they don't have to go through the same trials, or, in more positive experiences, to impart "nuggets of wisdom."

MENTORING

Paul Baltes, who was lauded for his groundbreaking work on the psychology of wisdom, and his colleague, Jacqui Smith, emphasized there is not just one ideal path to wisdom. The life experiences of wise individuals differ markedly, and so too the meaning and lessons they glean from them. They suggested that being mentored and observing how wise individuals deal with difficulties can develop wisdom. "A lot of wisdom can be gained from observing wise individuals as they deal with life matters" (Glück 2022, 177).

Several studies that have asked participants to suggest how wisdom develops have found that mentoring from and learning from wise individuals are highly favored by respondents. One such study is by Drew Krafcik, resident fellow at Stanford University. He conducted an in-depth study of twenty wise individuals and found that 50 percent spoke of learning wisdom through mentors and teachers as role models, by observing how mentors and teachers live, and attempting to practice what they observe.

One of Krafcik's research participants made the following comment:

> The best way to learn it is to hang out with wise people… You become wise when you spend time with somebody who has some wisdom. And just that consistency of relating for a period of time, you get to know how people think and how they respond and so forth (Krafcik 2015, 15).

Another said:

> [Wisdom] can be taught, but people need to do the work themselves… the way can be pointed out, and the path of practice can be pointed out, but real wisdom develops only when we actually do the work (Krafcik 2015, 18).

I think the crucial point this research participant is making is that wisdom can only really develop through making sense of our own experiences, not those of others. It reminds me of a Confucian quote: "By three methods we may learn wisdom: First, by reflection, which is noblest. Second, by imitation, which is easiest. And third by experience, which is the bitterest."

Perhaps future research should consider how the wise might pass on wisdom to others through mentoring. I know from my own experience of being mentored and mentoring others that it is time-consuming, but then again, isn't growing in wisdom a lifelong journey?

When I interviewed Judith Glück, who researches how wisdom can develop, she was quite clear that becoming wiser is not always a pleasant experience, and not everyone grows wise with age or experience. She noted, "Wisdom seems to be the result of a rare developmental process that involves a complex interaction of motivational, affective, and cognitive capacities… challenging life experiences and profound interactions with others."

Despite the many paths one can take, few people actually find wisdom. In my introductory chapter, Monika Ardelt said, "The road to becoming wise is long, arduous, and involves many hours of self-reflection." Perhaps the immediate access we have to almost anything we desire has ruined our ability to engage in the kind of reflection that would help us grow in wisdom. Are we, perhaps, too impatient to become wise?

Grace's story revealed some forty years of reflection to make sense of her trials, "and will continue," she says, "until there is no breath or energy left to be curious and to learn." What is clear from Grace's story, and from decades of research on the psychology of wisdom, is there is a critical step that cannot be by-passed on the way to becoming wise: It is the acquisition of self-knowledge. As Aristotle said, "Knowing yourself is the beginning of all wisdom."

Once the foundation work of self-understanding has reached a certain stage, it mediates the processes of dealing with, making sense of, and learning from one's life experiences. When we become more understanding and accepting of our own faults, we can be more accepting of the shortcomings of others. The discipline of developing a quiet ego and transcending the self is believed by many experts to be a necessity on the path to growing in wisdom. I close with Ardelt's words: "Ninety-nine percent of us do have an ego, but maybe we can quiet it down a little bit every day, and in so doing we can all be on the path toward self-transcendence."

CHAPTER EIGHT

WISDOM IN ACTION

On the sullen, wet Thursday evening of September 8, 2022, the United Kingdom received tragic news: The British Monarch, Queen Elizabeth II, had died at the age of ninety-six. A figurehead of stability for seven decades, she was the longest-serving British monarch (Royal website).

Elizabeth Alexandra Mary Windsor was born on April 21, 1926, in Mayfair, London, the first child of the Duke and Duchess of York (later King George VI and Queen Elizabeth). Her father ascended to the throne in 1936 upon the abdication of his brother, King Edward VIII, making Elizabeth the heir apparent (Zatz 2023).

She and her husband, Prince Philip, were on a State visit to Kenya because her father was too ill to undertake the visit himself. At 14:45 on February 6, 1952, Prince Philip took his twenty-five-year-old wife for a walk in the garden to share the news her father had died. The Princess had become queen of the United Kingdom, Northern Ireland, and the Commonwealth States whilst on this stately visit (Zatz 2023; The Guardian).

Consider the Shakespearean quote: "Some are born great, some achieve greatness, and others have greatness thrust upon them" (William Shakespeare, Twelfth Night, Act II, Scene 5).

It might appear from the facts of her lineage Queen Elizabeth II had "greatness thrust upon" her at the age of twenty-five. However, when one views historical television footage throughout the decades of her reign, it looks more like she was "born great." She had incredible poise and presence. As she matured and grew more confident in her role, I thought of her as a wise stateswoman. She spoke with confidence and authority. But more than that, there was a certain forethought in her messages. They carried hope, encouragement, and inspiration. Although she was the most visually represented person in the world and her influence vast, she never flaunted her status.

During the Queen's seventy-year reign, fifteen UK prime ministers and numerous heads of commonwealth states sought out and benefited from her counsel. No doubt she also influenced many other visiting heads of state, presidents and so on. The British Broadcasting Corporation (BBC) asked six of the fifteen prime ministers about what they had gleaned from their regular meetings with the Queen.

They said of her, "There was always a wise word to be had." "She was considerate, caring, endlessly patient." "She had a great sense of humour." "Wanted to put people at their ease." "Of all the leaders, of all the heads of state I met, Queen Elizabeth II was the most impressive." "It was a privilege to be able to call on her sage advice and wise counsel" (BBC 2022).

Some may say they don't think Queen Elizabeth was wise because she did this or she didn't do that, but they should remember, no one can be wise in all things all of the time.

Of all the positions where we might expect to see and hear wisdom, none is more visible than leadership. Leaders in government run our countries, in religion our churches, in education our schools and universities, and in business our companies. Daily, we are exposed, in some shape or form, to their messages, values, and decisions. Much as we might expect wisdom from people in leadership positions, there is too little in evidence. That is not to say there is none, but I have long been puzzled by how little effort is made by organizations to harvest wisdom from those who demonstrate it before they retire to pass it on to younger employees.

Some years ago, whilst engaged in a senior executive development initiative, I met Jack. Jack clearly exhibited wisdom and was nearing retirement. I spoke to the CEO, gained his immediate support, and implemented a coach-mentoring program such that Jack would meet with each of the leaders to impart what he had learned from his years of experience. He proved to be a natural mentor, giving each leader tips and nuggets of wisdom to practice until their next meeting when they would review and enhance. Programs such as this are simple to put in place and, if maintained, enhance the overall wisdom of the organization over time and serve to develop wisdom in leaders, extant and prospective, earlier in their careers than if left to chance.

This chapter is about how some extraordinary people have demonstrated wisdom but will also give an example of its antithesis. I include both to illustrate that, whether for good or bad, the decisions and actions of people in positions of influence tend to impact others way beyond their immediate circle. I address four spheres of activity where wisdom is needed: education, family, business, and government.

EDUCATION

To illustrate how interrelated these spheres are, here is the story of an icon of education who fought vigorously to change the worldviews of governments on education.

Kenneth Robinson was born on March 4, 1950, in Liverpool, England. He was one of seven children from a working-class background. Robinson contracted polio at age four, which didn't seem to hold him back (Bates 2020). Google him and you will find his TED talk, "Do Schools Kill Creativity?" is ranked the most highly viewed since its delivery in 2006.

He was professor of arts education at the University of Warwick in the UK and later professor emeritus. In 1999, he led a national commission on creativity, education, and the economy for the UK Government, the findings of which were published in "The Robinson Report." He is the author of several books and was considered by *Fast*

Company magazine as one of "the world's elite thinkers on creativity and innovation." In 2003, he received a knighthood from Queen Elizabeth II for his services to the arts (Bates 2020).

Robinson worked internationally for decades to release the creative energies of children, adults, and organizations. He led national and international projects on creative and cultural education in the United States, the UK, Europe, and Asia (Ken Robinson's website).

In this very thought-provoking TED talk, he airs his views on how the education system is geared to kill the natural creativity that appears in all of us during childhood. He strongly asserts that creativity should have the same status as literacy in schools and that we should treat it with the same gravity. He believes all kids have tremendous talent, and "we squander them ruthlessly." It appears the very system meant to edify them seems also to be the one that limits them (Ted 2006).

One of my highlights of his talk is the lovely story of a six-year-old girl in a drawing lesson. He reported that she'd hardly ever paid attention, but in this drawing lesson she did. "The teacher, fascinated, went over to her, and said, 'What are you drawing?' And the girl said, 'I'm drawing a picture of God.' And the teacher said, 'But nobody knows what God looks like.' And the girl said, 'They will in a minute'" (Ted 2006). This was testimony to the fearlessness and lack of inhibitions that children have. They are not afraid of being wrong. He then made a statement that I think speaks volumes and is a challenge to all of us: "If you're not prepared to be wrong, you'll never come up with anything original!" (Ted 2006).

I agree with Robinson that by the time kids reach adulthood, they have become afraid of being wrong. He asserts: "We need to radically rethink our view of intelligence. We need to rethink the fundamental principles on which we're educating our children. We get educated out of our creativity" (Ted 2006).

What I like about Robinson's out-of-the-box thinking is that he's bold, he's imaginative, he's profoundly challenging in his presentation of reality. Sadly, he passed away in 2020, but his final book, *Imagine If... Creating a Future for Us All*, which encapsulates his manifesto, was published posthumously by his daughter, Kate (Robinson's website). Robinson wanted governments to think about education systems differently, not ditching curricula but, instead of solely prioritizing academic achievement and conformity, liberate children's imaginations and initiative.

His friend and agent Brendan Barns wrote about him: "What really set Ken apart from other speakers and educationists was his ability instantly to create rapport with his audiences. He made everyone feel he was talking to them personally" (Bates 2020). I'm not suggesting Ken Robinson was wise, but the ease with which he pushed the boundaries of conventionality, his clever sense of humor, and his efforts to benefit so many make me wonder.

Robert J. Sternberg, professor of human development at Cornell University, is also an advocate of revamping the priorities of the education system and curricula to include the teaching of wisdom. He and his colleagues, Alina Reznitskaya, professor of educational foundations, Montclair State University, New Jersey, and Linda Jarvin, president of Paris College of Art, France, noted, "Education has taken the easier, quicker route. It leads students rapidly and relatively smoothly—in the wrong direction" (Sternberg, Reznitskaya, and Jarvin 2007, 144).

Sternberg and his colleagues regard the wrong direction to be "illustrated by the high-stakes systems of testing," which are part of most school curricula. The education system rewards individuals who obtain high scores on IQ tests, SATs, and the like. This takes a narrow view of intelligence. As a result, schools are unlikely to teach anything that does not promise to raise conventional test scores (Sternberg, Reznitskaya, and Jarvin 2007, 144)

I don't know if Robinson and Sternberg knew each other, but they certainly sang from the same hymn sheet. Robinson wanted to redesign the education system so it incorporated multiple intelligences—intelligences that are diverse, dynamic, and constantly evolving, not just mental arithmetic. Sternberg wanted to infuse the school curriculum with "wisdom-related instruction," which "teaches children not *what* to think, but, rather, *how* to think" (Sternberg, Reznitskaya, and Jarvin 2007, 151).

Perhaps, if Robinson and Sternberg had been able to combine their efforts, they might have been able to achieve much more than each did individually. Both realized the critical importance of our formative years to what and how we learn and in the creation of an appetite for life-long learning. Much of what we learn in our younger years is through engaging with our families. I had the privilege of growing up with my maternal grandfather, Petrus. Most who knew him would agree he was an extremely smart man, but was he wise? Let me share something of his story with you, and you can judge for yourself.

FAMILY

My grandfather was an extremely intelligent and gifted man. He was born in 1915, during the height of the seg-regationist policies in South Africa, prior to their enact-ment in 1948. If he were born at a time and in a place where opportunities were equal for all races, his life might have taken a very different turn. He often said to me he wished he'd had the opportunity to go to university to study engineering. People of color were not able to attend universities or be formally educated at that time. In con-sequence, my grandfather trained as an "unqualified engi-neer" with the local council working as an apprentice to his white supervisors. During his time at the council, he was highly praised for his innovations and was presented with several awards for finding smarter and more cost-ef-fective ways in which the council could work.

Reflecting on his life, one of the things that my grand-father did that truly impressed me was how he started his own transport business whilst working at the council. The public transport system in the poorer areas where we lived was atrocious, and people found it difficult to get to work. The company where my uncles worked was punitive. Regarding late coming, pay was docked for late arrivals. So, my grandfather bought a passenger carrier vehicle and enlisted two of his sons, who worked shifts at the company, to take turns to drive their fellow workmates to and from work for the same fee they would spend on the buses.

The passengers benefited because they were being picked up at home and dropped off at work on time. This resulted in them earning their full wage, so gaining financially. They arrived home earlier, so their home lives improved because of less stress and more quality time with their families. In consequence, they were happier, which enhanced their home lives and those of their families. Their greater happiness, in turn, increased their productivity at work.

My uncles profited because they got paid for driving the vehicle and didn't have to pay bus fare any longer. Each became a shareholder in the business, and in time, each got to own the vehicle he was driving. Also, their social connection with their passengers was strengthened, making for a more resilient and cohesive unit at work. My grandfather gained financially and, now that I understand more about wisdom, I think he also grew psychologically. I remember when the people whose lives were positively affected by his initiative approached him to ask if he could accommodate additional routes to service more passengers. He was overwhelmed by the good his little transport initiative had had on their lives.

He went on to purchase four vehicles in all and enlisted two men from among the passengers to become drivers. He was a pioneer, an entrepreneur, a great man with a permanently curious and inquiring mind. One of the most profound things he ever said to me was: "Always keep company with and listen to people who are older and wiser than you and stay away from people who are foolish." I've carried this with me all my life, and it has stood me in good stead.

My grandfather was smart, but he was smart with humility. He didn't flaunt it. Instead, he channeled it to be creative and make suggestions for improvement. It allowed him to see an opportunity where people were not getting to work on time, their pay was being docked, and their families were financially and socially penalized as a result. He penetrated beyond the surface of a problem to its essentials, as wise people do, and his solutions benefited multiple constituents. Time and again, he demonstrated wisdom in action.

That was his way, constantly looking to improve things, circumstances, aware of his present situation but anticipating the future. That's how I remember him; always discerning what might happen next and turning problems, real and potential, into opportunities.

I think wisdom is about taking action that has the capacity to benefit many, not just a few. What follows is a great example of how one leader's behavior positively contributed to enhancing the lives of those in his organization and their families.

BUSINESS

In 1980, Max De Pree became the CEO of Herman Miller, Inc. (high-end furniture company) (Damon 2004, 24). During his tenure, Herman Miller became one of the most profitable Fortune 500 companies. De Pree is credited with turning a small family-owned business into what was, at the time, the second largest furniture maker in the world. In 1983, it was chosen as one of "the 100 best companies to work for in America" (De Pree 1989, xii), and in 1988, a Fortune poll picked Herman Miller as one of the nation's "ten most admired companies... first in its industry... fourth out of all US companies in the category of 'quality of products or services.'" (De Pree 1989, xviii-xix).

But that's not what makes Herman Miller so special. Here's why: One hundred percent of all employees who have at least one year's tenure own company stock, and over 50 percent regularly purchase shares in addition to those that come as a benefit of employment. In other words, the employees have skin in the game.

Early in his tenure as CEO, De Pree convinced the board to introduce an employee stock-ownership plan, sharing a part of its capital wealth with its workers. William Damon, professor of education at Stanford University, interviewed De Pree (circa 2004) for his book, *The Moral Advantage*. During the interview, he was told: "One of the things that I'm most proud of is that almost everybody at Herman Miller is a stockholder" (Damon 2004, 25). During the interview, De Pree recounted a story of running into one of his former factory employees at a drugstore. The man said to De Pree that he had been planning on giving him a call to tell him he will be enjoying the kind of retirement he never dreamed was possible because De Pree made him a stockholder. De Pree then said to Damon, "I never gave him anything; he earned it all. The stock they get, they can buy at a discount, but the quarterly profit-sharing is paid in stock, since we're a public company" (Damon 2004, 25).

De Pree's behavior demonstrates wisdom. At the helm of the organization, he did not seek to flaunt the power and status of his position through self-aggrandizing actions, as many leaders do when they become CEO. Instead, he was more interested in enhancing the lives of everyone in the company, creating a culture where everyone had the same goals because all were owners.

Wise people are known to seek the common good, not just for those in their immediate circle but in the world at large (Sternberg, Glück, and Karami 2022, 55). They care for others and show their concern by their actions, not just their words. Not to put too fine a point on it, but Max De Pree must have been extremely approachable if, as mentioned in his interview with Damon, the factory employee thought nothing of planning to call the retired CEO. Can you think of many successful retired CEOs who would take a call from someone from the junior ranks of the organization they once ran?

De Pree saw the shareholding idea as growing naturally out of his deep respect for all the company's employees. His leadership philosophy was one where the leader learns from direct reports just as they learn from the leader. A company's prosperity depends on this capacity to learn in both directions, from leader to followers and vice versa (De Pree 1989). Anne Colby and William Damon, both developmental psychologists, studied contemporary moral exemplars for their book, *Some Do Care*. They explored the lives and moral development of twenty-three men and women who have provided moral leadership in communities across the United States. Their findings, which surprised them, mirrored the leadership philosophy practiced by De Pree. They said, "We found moral leadership to be a back-and-forth, two-way street, much like the kind of 'interaction' that De Pree describes in the servant-as-leader approach to business management" (Damon 2004, 27).

De Pree credits his mentor, the late industrial psychologist Carl Frost, professor emeritus of psychology at Michigan State University and adviser to Herman Miller, with having imparted managerial wisdom to him (Damon 2004, 27). When De Pree was still a young manager, Dr. Carl Frost told him: "When you have problems running a factory and you don't know what to do, you go out in the factory and you ask the people who are working in the factory... they always know what to do, but nobody ever asks them" (Damon 2004, 27). De Pree took the advice and discovered that it worked. Max De Pree believed one should "abandon oneself to the strengths of others" (De Pree 1989, 9).

The wisdom literature from Socrates through to the present day is replete with reference to knowing and accepting the limitations of your own knowledge. No one can have all the answers all the time, but many leaders are disinclined to ask their people for their opinions, feedback, or suggestions, for fear it would somehow undermine their power, control, and authority. Leaders do not lose by showing humility. Rather, they enhance their standing and authenticity. By much the same token, a leader can gain by giving of themselves, their time, talents, and advice to others.

"The first responsibility of a leader is to define reality. The last is to say thank you. In between the two, the leader must become a servant and a debtor."

—MAX DE PREE (1989, 11)

He believed the leader is the "servant" of his followers, removing obstacles that inhibit them from doing their jobs. Moreover, "the true leader enables followers to realize their full potential" (De Pree 1989, xx).

Max De Pree was an outstanding leader and an admirable human being. The legacy he leaves is a stellar example of how others could do the same. Many of the business principles he advocated and lived by exemplify wise behavior. De Pree was an innovator with immense integrity and a great deal of humility.

"I've learned that people will forget what you said, people will forget what you did, but people will never forget how you made them feel."

—MAYA ANGELOU, AMERICAN POET, SINGER, MEMOIRIST, AND CIVIL RIGHTS ACTIVIST

These words apply in every walk of life. School children remember teachers who treated them well and, consequently, go on to study that particular subject at university. People leave jobs not because of compensation but because of their direct manager's behavior. Here is an example of malign governmental influence.

GOVERNMENT
On the afternoon of September 6, 1966, the sixty-four-year-old architect of apartheid, Dr. Hendrik F. Verwoerd, was assassinated by Dimitri Tsafendas, a Greek-Mozam-bican parliamentary messenger who hadn't attracted attention from security staff because he was in his official uniform. As news of the killing became known, Daniel A. Gross, American journalist and public radio producer, wrote, "The architect was dead, but his policies were not; the system that Verwoerd helped to establish would continue to subjugate black South Africans for almost three decades" (Gross 2016).

More than five decades since his assassination and nearly three decades since apartheid was abandoned, Verwoerd's name still carries a hugely negative symbolism for the vast majority of South Africans. Moreover, the legacy of his laws reverberates in a country still very much divided by economic inequalities and race.

Hendrik Frensch Verwoerd was born in Amsterdam, the Netherlands, on September 8, 1901. In 1903, his family moved to South Africa because of his father's sympathy toward the Afrikaner nation (Dutch settlers) after the

South African War. Verwoerd was considered extremely bright. In his final school year exams, he came first in his province (Orange Free State) and fourth in South Africa. He is reported to have received both his masters and doctorate in philosophy from the University of Stellenbosch with distinction, where he later held academic posts first in psychology and later in sociology and social work between 1924 through to 1936 (Overcoming Apartheid, MSU).

Verwoerd was clearly an extremely intelligent man, but history certainly does not judge him to have been wise. In chapter one, I discussed the differences between intelligence and wisdom. One of those differences is that intelligence can be used for good or for evil, but wisdom is never the latter. Verwoerd provides us an excellent example of this distinction. Others whose names you will be familiar with are Adolf Hitler and Joseph Stalin.

In chapter five, I pointed out that we prioritize those things to which we attach value and our behavior flows from what we value; wise individuals' values are focused on a greater good to balance the interests of all parties concerned. All too often, we see media reports about people in leadership positions, whose conduct should be an example to others, behaving as though they are above the rules; the rules don't apply to them.

The purposes of government should be to ensure security, maintain social order, and provide public services. This is achieved by those in government exercising the powers bestowed upon them by making and implementing laws. But for this to work effectively, these powers must be used to the benefit of all, not to the benefit of just a few, and not just for immediate effect but with some thought to the future. The very nature of government and their actions must inevitably impact the nature and course of people's lives. It follows, then, that those we place in government, and in other positions of influence and leadership, should be selected from those who demonstrate wisdom, not just intelligence and certainly not self-interest.

> *"Government remains the paramount field of unwisdom because it is there that men seek power over others—only to lose it over themselves"* *—Barbara Tuchman, historian and two-time Pulitzer Prize winning author (Hall 2010, 258)*

Have you ever noticed that many people who ascend to leadership positions tend to crave the power that comes with that position, rather than desire such a position because of the beneficial impact it can have on the many? When I was looking for senior business leaders to participate in my doctoral work, which explored their psychological development, one of my colleagues in the US was looking for people from all walks of life to try to find highly psychologically evolved individuals. When we compared notes, I mentioned I couldn't find many in the top echelons of UK businesses. She told me that I wouldn't, that these people are not in business. I asked her where they are. Her answer was quite emphatic: "These people don't want to be in power, they just want to do good. If we're lucky, we might find them running charities."

This observation is consistent with the twenty-three contemporary moral exemplars interviewed by Colby and Damon, who comprised people who worked for the poor, fought for civil rights, and dedicated their lives to the good of others.

Damon cautions leaders with regards the power that comes with their position. He says, "One of the essentials of good leadership is keeping perspective on the power that your position grants you. The best way to do this is to remember that the power is in the position, not in your own intrinsic superiority to others; and that it is a power meant to serve others, not to dominate them" (Damon 2004, 26).

In this chapter, I have described examples which encapsulate the words of Caroline Bassett, founder of The Wisdom Institute, Minneapolis, that "wisdom lies on a continuum... from the extraordinary to the everyday" (Bassett 2011, 304). We have seen examples from a queen who, by virtue of her position, had extraordinary reach and influence; Sir Ken Robinson whose incredible passion invited millions to view his TED talks; through to my grandfather, Petrus, whose impact was very much more community based; and Max De Pree, who didn't just do business as usual but demonstrated that leadership and wisdom is about service to others. By way of contrast, I have included an example of one monumental governmental failure, Dr. Hendrik Verwoerd.

By now you have probably thought of examples of those who have demonstrated wisdom and those who have not.

The challenge, however, is not whether we can find examples of wisdom but whether we find sufficient, and if not, what can we, individually and collectively, do about it?

CONCLUDING COMMENTS

"No man ever steps in the same river twice, for it's not the same river and he's not the same man."

—HERACLITUS, GREEK PHILOSOPHER, CIRCA 500 BCE

If you have ever written a nonfiction book, you will know it is a journey, where knowledge evolves and the way you interpret things changes constantly. My hope is that, as you have journeyed through this book with me, you too have experienced a shift in your knowledge and understanding of wise behavior. I invite you to join me on a final walk through this book as I share with you the things that have captivated me, some of which have challenged me to change my own behavior.

Jane Goodall bursts onto the scene in chapter one with her powerful, timeless quote about our loss of wisdom and lack of concern for future generations. Erik Erikson made a very similar observation twenty years prior to

Goodall—no change there for humanity. I, like Goodall, am saddened our actions still seem to show very little concern for future generations. We do need to practice more generativity as a priority. We need to ask ourselves what we can do to increase our acts of generativity. What can we do differently to show more regard for our future generations and the future of our planet?

It was a real honor to interview Dr. Dilip V. Jeste for chapter two and to hear the remarkable story of how he came to study geriatric neuropsychiatry. His ground-breaking work on where wisdom processing is located in the human brain has given wisdom, as an area of research, a surge in credibility. In his book, *Wiser*, he reveals the work he and his colleagues continue to do to further the field of the neuroscience of wisdom. I highly recommend his book if you would like to know more.

Two things about chapter three particularly appealed to me. The first was the heroine of the chapter, Frances Oldham Kelsey, who prevented a dangerous drug from impacting the lives of countless people globally. We can learn a great deal from her behavior, for instance, she didn't give in to "Big Pharma" when it tried to intimidate her. How many people do you know would take a stand against corporate America? Kelsey pushed accepted standards beyond the conventional to create new standards for the way drugs are approved in the US and globally.

The second thing that appealed to me was the excellent way the late Jacob W. Getzels illustrates that when you ask the right questions, you enhance the quality of the solutions. Perhaps we could all think more carefully about whether we're asking the right questions before we launch into solution mode.

Among the many things I learned about wisdom from studying the life of Nelson Mandela was that humor and wisdom are often inextricably connected. Wise people often use humor to make their points and soften the blow of hard truths. Nelson Mandela will forever be remembered for the way he transformed the lives of future generations in South Africa. He epitomizes wisdom the world over, a symbol of peace and reconciliation, which is what made me think of him as an exemplar in chapter four. When most people are asked to describe Mandela, they probably won't think of his humor. Yet Blake Bromley, international charity lawyer, did. He said his "dominant memory" was of Mandela's humor. Mandela, said Bromley, "used humor as a subtle tool to diffuse confrontations before they turned ugly or violent."

It never occurred to me before writing about wise people that they use humor so cleverly. I was pleasantly surprised at how often humor surfaced in the behavior of the wise. The few wise people I know use humor to lighten many a tense moment. Jeffrey Dean Webster, a wisdom researcher, thought it significant enough to include in his wisdom model. Perhaps you don't think you have a great sense of humor, but take a look around you and notice those individuals who do, and see how they use it and what for. It might be quite illuminating.

While researching this book, I came across a number of things that gave me pause for thought. The concept of "enlightened self-interest" has been one of the highlights of my journey. When psychologist Jeremy Frimer and his colleagues wrote about Rosa Parks as a moral exemplar, chapter five was a fitting place for her story. Rosa merged her self-interests with the interests of others. I have read about wise people balancing their own interests with the interests of others but have not heard it referred to as enlightened self-interest by wisdom researchers. I thought this was an excellent description of the behavior.

Whilst researching and writing chapter six, my understanding of wise behavior was considerably enhanced. I learned not just any kind of reflection will lead to wise insights, but exploratory reflection (going deeper into the meaning of the event) leads to growth in wisdom.

Another discovery was the concept of a "quiet ego," which transcends self-focused, self-centered behavior, not by neglecting the self but rather by balancing concern for self with concern for others. This resonated with the concept of enlightened self-interest (in chapter five). What's more, someone with a quiet ego exhibits values of self-transcendence, benevolence, universalism, and self-direction (independent thought and action—choosing, creating, exploring). Wayment and Bauer, who coined the term the "quiet ego," suggest that to quiet one's ego, a focus on one's important values may help to reduce one's sense of threat and defensiveness (2018,

12). These values just happen to be the same as those associated with wise people.

Another insight came from Paul Wong's conception of self-transcendence, which he views as a journey or process in which we are continuously improving to expand our potential. But here's the key: This journey is not in service of self but in service to others. This got me thinking that if we quiet our egos, practice humility, and transcend self-focus so we become more other-focused, doesn't service to others evolve naturally, and isn't this the path to wise behavior?

Grace, the star of chapter seven, had a horrific start to her life, but with the help of counseling, finding her own faith, mentoring from wise individuals, and a loving family of her own, she eventually found freedom, healing, and growth in wisdom. Grace's story provides many insights into wise behavior, but what really stood out for me were two things: trying to understand that those who hurt others have most likely suffered some form of harm themselves; and forgiveness. I didn't delve into the concept of forgiveness, but I do think it's an important one for psychological well-being and, probably, for psychological evolution. Grace got me wondering whether wise people are able to forgive relatively more easily. Does the exploratory reflection wise people practice perhaps help with forgiveness? Does exploratory reflection increase our awareness not only of ourselves but of the pain and circumstances of others? Does it enable us to appreciate a bigger picture?

Can being on a growth-pathway enhance our capacity to forgive others?

Queen Elizabeth II, the longest serving British monarch, died whilst I was writing this book. She had inspired me with her gentle yet powerful demeanor, her humility, and a life dedicated to serving others. It seemed fitting to open chapter eight with a tribute to her indelible legacy. This chapter showcased some others who have displayed exceptional behavior. It was also to remind us about the devastating and enduring impact of unwise action, such as those of the architect of apartheid in South Africa, Dr. Hendrik Verwoerd. I hope I succeeded in showing that, whether for good or bad, the decisions and actions of people in positions of power and influence impact others way beyond the immediate.

In chapter one, I wrote about the people I interviewed and how I asked them, "Who is the wisest person you know, and why are they wise?" In their answers, they did not describe something or someone mythical, enigmatic, or perfect. They did not describe actions reserved only for wise exemplars, but actions you and I can strive toward in our daily lives if we so desire.

It is within the grasp of each of us, Homo sapiens, "wise man," to live up to our name. In my introduction, I suggested that instead of focusing solely on one's own issues and those in one's immediate circle to perhaps look further afield and, in so doing, help those who are in need. Perhaps, in reading this book, you have been sufficiently challenged to think more about how you might grow your own capacity for making wise decisions and whether you might leave a more impactful legacy that will live on to benefit future generations.

I hope you have been moved to take up the challenge and feel inspired to start your own journey to becoming wise.

ACKNOWLEDGMENTS

I am delighted to give thanks to those who have helped make this journey doable and, above all, have encouraged my progress to completion.

My husband, best-friend, and soulmate, I cannot begin to thank you enough for the gift of your love, support, and tireless enthusiasm you show me daily. You always champion all my causes and, because you believe in me, I have believed I could complete this project. Since I began this book journey in June 2022, you have been a saint, spending your evenings and weekends alone. I have much to make up for, and may I start by saying how truly grateful I am that you are in my life!

My mother, Lydia Johannes, whose strength of character and tenacity encouraged me never to settle, but to reach for those things I most wanted and desired.

My editor, Trisha Giramma, you deserve more praise than my vocabulary will allow. You have taken my writing to a completely different level, one I did not know I had in me. Thank you for all your support, guidance, and inspiration. This book wouldn't be what it is today if it wasn't for your first-class editing skills. You have also challenged my thinking. I suspect only great editors achieve this for their authors!

A special thanks to Professor Judith Glück for being so extremely generous with your time and providing me with such invaluable feedback and enthusiasm, which has significantly enhanced the quality of those chapters. It has been an honor to have someone of your caliber comment on my novice attempt at writing a book on your expert subject. With gratitude and appreciation, thank you!

To my dedicated and talented beta readers: Caroline Buchan, Jamie Corbin, Eileen Day, Kathryn Hathaway, Annemarié Oosthuizen, Andrea Palmer-Gray, John Saunders, and Victoria Shiroma Wilson. Thank you for the gift of your time and for your invaluable feedback that has raised the standard of my writing. I have tried to do justice to your insightful suggestions.

To the experts who gave of their busy lives to answer my questions: Monika Ardelt, Dilip V. Jeste, Bill R. Torbert, and Nic M. Weststrate. Thank you for your time, encouragement, and inspiration.

To Laura Elvia Hall for asking me the question that led to the writing of this book.

To my family and friends who have cheered me on and continued to fan my flame when I flagged.

To everyone at Manuscripts LLC and New Degree Press who work tirelessly behind the scenes to help make every author's journey special. Thank you. Your individual and combined efforts are making a difference.

Last, but not least, a special thanks to the individuals who gave their life stories to add substance to this book. I have learned a great deal about wisdom from hearing your stories. Your open and generous participation has significantly impacted the quality of this book.

In particular, thank you Agnes Morgan-Smith, now sadly deceased, who was a real pioneer of women's liberation forging her way in a man's world, and her daughter, Annemarié, who shared so generously with me her mother's story. To Eileen, my mentor, you are an incredible woman, and you continue to amaze me with your wisdom. To Dilip Jeste, who shared so open-heartedly his life story. The amazing Grace, who shared her remarkable story and breathed life into chapter seven. Last, but not least, my grandfather, whose legacy lives on in his extended family. I hope you enjoy what I've written about you!

APPENDIX

INTRODUCTION

Weststrate, Nic M. and Judith Glück. 2017. "Hard-earned wisdom: exploratory processing of difficult life experience is positively associated with wisdom." *Developmental Psychology*. 53. 800-814. 10.1037/dev0000286.

CHAPTER ONE

Ardelt, Monika. 2005. "How Wise People Cope with Crises and Obstacles in Life." *ReVision*, 28: 7-19.

Bassett, Caroline L. 2011. "Wisdom and its development: Learning to become wise(r)." 2011. In *The Oxford Handbook of Reciprocal Adult Development and Learning* (2nd Ed.) edited by Carol Hoare, 302-317. Oxford, UK: Oxford University Press.

BBC (British Broadcasting Corporation), January 4th 2023,
    "How microplastics are infiltrating the food you eat",
    Isabelle Gerretsen
    www.bbc.com/future/article/20230103-how-plastic-is-
    getting-into-our-food.

CHEMTrust, September 2019, "PFAS the 'Forever Chemicals' ",
    Dr Julie Schneider
    https://chemtrust.org/wp-content/uploads/PFAS_Brief_
    CHEMTrust_2019.pdf.

Clayton, Vivian. 1982. "Wisdom and intelligence: the nature
    and function of knowledge in the later years."
    The International Journal of Aging and Human Development.
    15, 4, 315-21. DOI: 10.2190/17tq-bw3y-p8j4-tg40. PMID: 7183572.

Gino, Francesca and Dan Ariely. 2012. "The dark
    side of creativity: Original thinkers can be more
    dishonest." *Journal of Personality and Social Psychology*, 102,
    3, 445–459.
    https://doi.org/10.1037/a0026406.

Glück, Judith and Andreas Scherpf. 2022. "Intelligence
    and wisdom: age-related differences and nonlinear
    relationships." *Psychology and Aging*, 37, 5, 649–666.
    https://doi.org/10.1037/pag0000692.

Goleman, Daniel. June 14, 1988. "Erikson, in His Own Old Age,
    Expands His View of Life." Accessed: 18th October 2022.
    https://archive.nytimes.com/www.nytimes.
    com/books/99/08/22/specials/erikson-old.
    html?scp=161&sq=old%2520people&st=Search.

Goodall, Jane in Andrew Zuckerman. 2008. "Wisdom." Edited by Alex Vlack. P.Q. Blackwell in association with Abrams, New York.

Grint, Keith. 2005. "Problems, problems, problems: The social construction of leadership." *Human Relations*, 58, 11, 1467-1494.

Hall, Stephen S. 2010. *Wisdom: From philosophy to neuroscience.* New York: Alfred A. Knopf.

Helson, R. and S. Srivastava. 2002. "Creative and wise people: Similarities, differences, and how they develop." *Personality and Social Psychology Bulletin*, 28, 1430-1440.

"Homo Sapiens." Encyclopedia.
Accessed: 18th October 2022.
https://www.encyclopedia.com/medicine/anatomy-and-physiology/anatomy-and-physiology/homo-sapiens.

Kitchener, K.S. and H.G. Brenner. 1990. "Wisdom and reflective judgment: Knowing in the face of uncertainty." In Robert J. Sternberg (Ed.), *Wisdom: Its nature, origins, and development*, 181-211. Cambridge, UK: Cambridge University Press.

NASA (National Aeronautics and Space Administration), March 2023, "Global Climate Change, Vital Signs, Carbon Dioxide."
https://climate.nasa.gov/vital-signs/carbon-dioxide.

NOAA (National Oceanic and Atmospheric Administration). 2022, "Climate Change: Atmospheric Carbon Dioxide," June 23, 2022. www.climate.gov/news-features/understanding-climate/climate-change-atmospheric-carbon-dioxide.

Rooney, David and Bernard McKenna. 2005. "Should the Knowledge-based Economy be a Savant or a Sage? Wisdom and Socially Intelligent Innovation," *Prometheus*, 23, 3, 307-323, DOI: 10.1080/08109020500211025.

Rooney, David, Bernard McKenna, Peter Liesch, and Kim Boal. 2008. *The SAGE Handbook of New Approaches in Management and Organization*. London: SAGE Publications Ltd. 344-346. https://doi.org/10.4135/9781849200394.

Simonton, Dean K. 2002. "Creativity." In C. R. Snyder & S. J. Lopez (Eds.), *Handbook of positive psychology* 189–201. Oxford: Oxford University Press.

Sternberg, Robert J. 1986. "Intelligence, Wisdom, and Creativity: Three is Better Than One." *Educational Psychologist*, 21, 3, 175-190.

Sternberg, Robert J. 1998. "A Balance Theory of Wisdom." *Review of General Psychology*, 2, 4, 347–365.

Sternberg, Robert J. 2001. "What is the Common Thread of Creativity? Its Dialectical Relation to Intelligence and Wisdom." *The American psychologist*, 56, 360-362. DOI: 10.1037//0003-066X.56.4.360.

Sternberg, Robert J. 2017. "Developing the next generation of responsible professionals: Wisdom and ethics trump knowledge and IQ." *Psychology Teaching Review*, 23, 2, 51-59.

Sternberg, Robert J. 2019. "Race to Samarra: the critical importance of wisdom in the world today." In *The Cambridge handbook of wisdom,* edited by Robert J. Sternberg and Judith Glück, 551–574. Cambridge: Cambridge University Press.

Sternberg, Robert J. and Judith Glück. 2022. "Introduction: What is wisdom and why is it important?" In *The Psychology of Wisdom: An Introduction*, edited by Robert J. Sternberg and Judith Glück, 3-14. Cambridge: Cambridge University Press.

Sternberg, Robert J., Judith Glück, and Sareh Karami. 2022. "Psychological theories of wisdom." In *The Psychology of Wisdom: An Introduction*, edited by Robert J. Sternberg and Judith Glück, 53-69. Cambridge: Cambridge University Press.

UNDP (United Nations Development Programme), May 4 2021, "Short-termism—the greatest threat for our future?", Draško Drašković. https://www.undp.org/serbia/blog/short-termism-greatest-threat-our-future.

WEF (World Economic Forum), 2022, "The Global Risks Report 2022" (17th Edition) www3.weforum.org/docs/WEF_The_Global_Risks_Report_2022.pdf

CHAPTER TWO

Ardelt, Monika. 2003. "Empirical Assessment of a Three-Dimensional Wisdom Scale." *Research on Aging*, 25, 275-324. 10.1177/0164027503025003004.

Baltes, Paul B. and Jacqui Smith. 2008. "The fascination of wisdom: Its nature, ontogeny, and function." *Perspectives on psychological science*, 3, 1, 56-64.

Birren, James E., and C.M. Svensson. 2005. "Wisdom in history." In *A Handbook of Wisdom: Psychological Perspectives.* 3-31, edited by Robert J. Sternberg and Jennifer Jordan. Cambridge: Cambridge University Press.

Brugman Gerard M. 2006. "Wisdom and aging." In *Handbook of the Psychology of Aging*, edited by J.E. Birren, K.W. Schaie, and R.P. Abeles, 445–476. San Diego, CA: Academic

Jeste, Dilip V. and Scott LaFee. 2020. *Wiser: The scientific roots of wisdom, compassion, and what makes us good.* Boulder, Colorado: Sounds True.

Learning Without Scars. "Why Socrates..." June 29th 2020. Socratic Method. https://learningwithoutscars.com/socrates-says-blog/why-socrates/.

Mickler, Charlotte and Ursula Staudinger. 2009. "Personal Wisdom: Validation and Age-Related Differences of a Performance Measure." *Psychology and aging*, 23, 787-99. DOI: 10.1037/a0013928.

Schwartz, Barry and Kenneth E. Sharpe. 2019. "Practical
    Wisdom: What Aristotle Might Add to Psychology."
    In *The Cambridge Handbook of Wisdom*, edited by Robert
    J. Sternberg and Judith Glück, 226–248. Cambridge, UK:
    Cambridge University Press.

Staudinger, Ursula and Judith Glück. 2011. "Psychological
    Wisdom Research: Commonalities and Differences in
    a Growing Field." *Annual review of psychology*, 62, 215-41.
    DOI: 10.1146/annurev.psych.121208.131659.

Sternberg, Robert J.1990. Ed. *Wisdom: Its Nature, Origins, And
    Development*. Cambridge, UK: Cambridge University Press.

Sternberg, R. J. and Judith Glück. 2019. Eds. *The Cambridge
    Handbook of Wisdom*. Cambridge, UK: Cambridge
    University Press.

Sternberg, Robert. J. and Jennifer Jordan. 2005. Eds. *A
    handbook of wisdom: Psychological perspectives.* Cambridge,
    UK: Cambridge University Press.

Swartwood, Jason D. 2022. "Philosophical foundations for
    the study of wisdom." In *The Psychology of Wisdom: An
    Introduction*, edited by Robert J. Sternberg and Judith
    Glück, 15-34. Cambridge, UK: Cambridge University Press.

Swartwood, Jason D. and Valerie Tiberius. 2019.
    "Philosophical foundations of wisdom." In *The Cambridge
    handbook of wisdom,* edited by Robert J. Sternberg
    and Judith Glück, 10–39. Cambridge, UK: Cambridge
    University Press.

The Bhagavad Gita. The Annenberg Learner.
www.learner.org/series/invitation-to-world-
literature/the-bhagavad-gita/the-bhagavad-gita-map-
timeline/#:~:text=400%20BCE%20%2D%20400%20CE.

Twomey, Steve. January 2010. "Phineas Gage: Neuroscience's
Most Famous Patient. An accident with a tamping iron made
Phineas Gage history's most famous brain-injury survivor."
Smithsonian Magazine Online. Accessed: October 2022.
www.smithsonianmag.com/history/phineas-gage-
neurosciences-most-famous-patient-11390067/.

Webster, Jeffrey Dean. 2007. "Measuring the character
strength of wisdom." *International journal of aging &
human development*, 65, 2, 163-83. DOI:10.2190/AG.65.2.d.

Yao, Xinzhong. 2000. "An introduction to Confucianism."
Cambridge, UK: Cambridge University Press.

CHAPTER THREE

Arlin, Patricia Kennedy. 1990. "Wisdom: the art of problem
finding." Chapter. In *Wisdom: Its Nature, Origins, and
Development*, edited by Robert J. Sternberg, 230–43.
Cambridge, UK: Cambridge University Press.

Basseches, Michael A. 1984. *Dialectical thinking and adult
development.* Norwood, New Jersey: Ablex.

Bren, Linda. "Frances Oldham Kelsey: FDA Medical Reviewer Leaves Her Mark on History" FDA Consumer Magazine, March-April 2001. https://permanent.access.gpo.gov/lps1609/www.fda.gov/fdac/features/2001/201_kelsey.html.

Clayton, Vivian. 1982. "Wisdom and intelligence: the nature and function of knowledge in the later years." *The International Journal of Aging and Human Development.* 15, 4, 315-21. DOI: 10.2190/17tq-bw3y-p8j4-tg40. PMID: 7183572.

Dillon, James T. 1983. "Problem finding and solving." *Journal of Creative Behavior*, 16, 2, 97-111.

Getzels, Jacob W. 1982. "The problem of the problem." In *The framing of questions and the consistency of response, new directions for methodology of social and behavioral science,* edited by R. Hogarth, 37-49. San Francisco, CA: Jossey-Bass.

Glück, Judith and Nic M. Weststrate. 2022. "The Wisdom Researchers and the Elephant: An Integrative Model of Wise Behavior." *Personality and Social Psychology Review*, 26, 4, 342–374. https://doi.org/10.1177/10888683221094650.

Kramer, Deirdre A. 1990. "Conceptualizing wisdom: the primacy of affect–cognition relations." In *Wisdom: Its Nature, Origins, and Development*, edited by Robert J. Sternberg, 279-314. Cambridge: Cambridge University Press.

Kunzmann, Ute. 2022. "The wisdom in emotions." In *The Psychology of Wisdom: An Introduction*, edited by Robert J. Sternberg and Judith Glück, 157-171. Cambridge, UK: Cambridge University Press.

Mackworth, Norman H. in Arlin, Patricia Kennedy. 1990. "Wisdom: the art of problem finding." Chapter. In *Wisdom: Its Nature, Origins, and Development*, edited by Robert J. Sternberg, 230–243. Cambridge: Cambridge University Press.

Sternberg, Robert J. 1998. "A Balance Theory of Wisdom." *Review of General Psychology*, 2, 4, 347–365.

Sternberg, Robert J. 2001. "What is the Common Thread of Creativity? Its Dialectical Relation to Intelligence and Wisdom." *American psychologist,* 56, 4, 360-362. 10.1037//0003-066X.56.4.360.

Sternberg, Robert J., Judith Glück, and Sareh Karami. 2022. "Psychological theories of wisdom." In *The Psychology of Wisdom: An Introduction*, edited by Robert J. Sternberg and Judith Glück, 53-69. Cambridge: Cambridge University Press.

Thalidomide. December 11th 2019. Science Museum UK. www.sciencemuseum.org.uk/objects-and-stories/ medicine/thalidomide.

Wertheimer, Max in Arlin, Patricia Kennedy. 1990. "Wisdom: the art of problem finding." In *Wisdom: Its Nature, Origins, and Development*, edited by Robert J. Sternberg, 230–243. Cambridge, UK: Cambridge University Press.

Wonderlic, Inc. 2002. *Wonderlic Personnel Test & Scholastic Level Exam User's Manual*. Wonderlic, Inc. Libertyville, IL.

CHAPTER FOUR

Ardelt, Monika. 2005. "How Wise People Cope with Crises and Obstacles in Life." *ReVision*, 28, 1, Summer, 7-19.

Ardelt, Monika and Dilip V. Jeste. 2018. "Wisdom and Hard Times: The Ameliorating Effect of Wisdom on the Negative Association Between Adverse Life Events and Well-Being." *The journals of gerontology. Series B, Psychological sciences and social sciences*, 73, 8, 1374-1383. doi:10.1093/geronb/gbw137.

Batson, C. D., N. Ahmad, D.A. Lishner, and J.A. Tsang. 2002. "Empathy and altruism." In *Handbook of positive psychology,* edited by C. R. Snyder and S. J. Lopez, 485–498. Oxford, UK: Oxford University Press.

Birren, James E. and Laurel M. Fisher. 1990. "The elements of wisdom: overview and integration." In *Wisdom: Its nature, origins, and development*, edited by Robert J. Sternberg, 181-211. Cambridge, UK: Cambridge University Press.

Bromley Blake. 2014. "The Humor of Nelson Mandela." HuffPost Online. www.huffpost.com/entry/the-humor-of-nelson-mand_b_4402695.

Callahan, Jamie L., Michael G. Hasler, and Homer Tolson. 2005. "Perceptions of emotion expressiveness: Gender differences among senior executives." *Leadership & Organization Development Journal*, 26, 7, 512-528.

Cassell, E. J. 2002. "Compassion." In *Handbook of positive psychology,* edited by C. R. Snyder and S. J. Lopez, 434–445. Oxford, UK: Oxford University Press.

Cooper, Robert K. and Ayman Sawaf. 2000. Executive EQ: Emotional Intelligence in Business. London, UK: TEXERE Publishing Limited.

Damásio, António R. 1994. "Descartes' Error: Emotion, Reason, and the Human Brain." New York: G.P. Putnam.

Eisenberg Nancy and Paul A. Miller. 1987. "The Relation of Empathy to Prosocial and Related Behaviors." *Psychological Bulletin*, 101, 1, 91-119.

Frum, Barbara. (December 5, 2013). "Nelson Mandela explains how he avoids feelings of revenge." Duration: 00:45. CBC News. Accessed: January 2023. www.youtube.com/watch?v=Bwdzhm_24r0.

Frum, Barbara. (February 14, 1990). "In South Africa with Nelson Mandela." CBC Archives. Duration: 11:04. www.cbc.ca/player/play/2422671186.

Glück, Judith. 2022. "The Development of Wisdom." In *The Psychology of Wisdom: An Introduction*, edited by Robert J. Sternberg and Judith Glück, 175–192. Cambridge, UK: Cambridge University Press.

Glück Judith and Robert J. Sternberg. 2022. "Wisdom, morality, and ethics." In *The Psychology of Wisdom: An Introduction*, edited by Robert J. Sternberg and Judith Glück, 118–134. Cambridge, UK: Cambridge University Press.

Glück, Judith and Nic M. Weststrate. 2022. "The Wisdom Researchers and the Elephant: An Integrative Model of Wise Behavior." *Personality and Social Psychology Review*, 26, 4, 342–374. https://doi.org/10.1177/10888683221094650.

Gray, Jeremy R., Todd S. Braver, and Marcus E. Raichle. 2002. "Integration of emotion and cognition in the lateral prefrontal cortex." *Proceedings of the National Academy of Sciences of the United States of America*, 99, 6, 4115-20. DOI:10.1073/pnas.062381899.

Goetz, Jennifer L., Dacher Keltner, and Emiliana Simon-Thomas. 2010. "Compassion: An Evolutionary Analysis and Empirical Review." *Psychological Bulletin*, 136, 3, May, 351–374. doi:10.1037/a0018807.

Gross, James J. 1998. "The emerging field of emotion regulation: An integrative review." *Review of General Psychology*, 2, 3, 271–299. https://doi.org/10.1037/1089-2680.2.3.271.

Gross, James J. 2002. "Emotion regulation: affective, cognitive, and social consequences." *Psychophysiology*, 39, 3, 281–291. https://doi.org/10.1017/s0048577201393198.

Jeste, Dilip V., Monika Ardelt, Dan Blazer, Helena C. Kraemer, George Vaillant, and Thomas W. Meeks. 2010. "Expert consensus on characteristics of wisdom: a Delphi method study." *The Gerontologist*, 50, 5, 668–680. https://doi.org/10.1093/geront/gnq022.

Johnson, Scott. 2012. "A Visit to Robben Island, the Brutal Prison that Held Mandela, Is Haunting and Inspiring, Smithsonian Magazine Online. Accessed: August 2022. www.smithsonianmag.com/travel/robben-island-a-monument-to-courage-62697703/.

Kang, Sun-Mee and Phillip R. Shaver. 2004. "Individual differences in emotional complexity: Their psychological implications." *Journal of Personality*, 72, 4, 687-726.

Kramer, Deirdre A. 1990. "Conceptualizing wisdom: the primacy of affect–cognition relations." In *Wisdom: Its Nature, Origins, and Development*, edited by Robert J. Sternberg, 279–314. Cambridge, UK: Cambridge University Press.

Kramer, Deirdre. A. 2000. "Wisdom as a classical source of human strength: Conceptualization and empirical inquiry." *Journal of Social and Clinical Psychology,* 19, 1, 83–101. https://doi.org/10.1521/jscp.2000.19.1.83.

Lyster, Tracy 1996. "A nomination approach to the study of wisdom in old age." Doctoral Dissertation, Concordia University, Montreal, Quebec, Canada.

Michie, Susan and Janaki Gooty. 2005. "Values, emotions, and authenticity: Will the real leader please stand up?" *Leadership Quarterly,* 16, 3, 441-457.

Neff, Kristin D., Kristin L. Kirkpatrick, Stephanie S. Rude. 2007. "Self-compassion and adaptive psychological functioning." *Journal of Research in Personality.* 41. 139–154. DOI: 10.1016/j.jrp.2006.03.004.

Peplow, Gemma. October 31, 2021. "Thailand cave rescue: UK diver says boys were in 'mortal danger every second underwater' as he relives heroic mission." https://news.sky.com/story/thailand-cave-rescue-uk-diver-says-boys-were-in-mortal-danger-every-second-underwater-as-he-relives-heroic-mission-12446349.

Pienaar, Francois. (December 5, 2013). "Rugby star Francois Pienaar reflects on South Africa's historic win at the 1995 rugby World Cup and how it led to a life-long friendship with Nelson Mandela." CBS News.com. You Tube Video. Duration: 2:10. www.youtube.com/watch?v=8rBtis7IzF8.

Rose, Charlie. (January 12, 2013). "Morgan Freeman on playing Nelson Mandela." Duration: 06:02. Accessed: January 2023. https://www.youtube.com/watch?v=WYdm3NB1E00.

Rugby Rucker. 2022. "Three countries that have been banned from playing in the Rugby World Cup." https://www.ruck.co.uk/three-countries-that-have-been-banned-from-playing-in-the-rugby-world-cup/.

Walsh, Roger. 2015. "What is Wisdom? Cross-Cultural and Cross-Disciplinary Syntheses." *Review of General Psychology*, 19, 3, 278–293. https://doi.org/10.1037/gpr0000045.

Webster, Jeffrey Dean. 2007. "Measuring the character strength of wisdom." *International journal of aging & human development*, 65, 2, 163-83. doi:10.2190/AG.65.2.d.

CHAPTER FIVE

Agar, John. March 24, 2011. "Dad who mistakenly gave 7-year-old son 'hard' lemonade at Tigers game sues after boy is taken away." https://www.mlive.com/news/2011/03/dad_who_mistakenly_gave_7-year.html.

Colby, Anne and William Damon. 1992. *Some do care: Contemporary lives of moral commitment.* New York, NY: The Free Press.

Damon, William. 2004. *The Moral Advantage: how to succeed in business by doing the right thing.* San Francisco, California: Berrett-Koehler Publishers, Inc.

Frimer, Jeremy A. and Lawrence J. Walker. 2009. "Reconciling the self and morality: an empirical model of moral centrality development." *Developmental psychology*, 45, 6, 1669-81.

Frimer, Jeremy A., Lawrence J. Walker, William Dunlop, Brenda Lee, and Amanda Riches. 2011. "The Integration of Agency and Communion in Moral Personality: Evidence of Enlightened Self-Interest." *Journal of personality and social psychology*, 101, 1, 149-163. DOI: 10.1037/a0023780.

Frimer, Jeremy A., Lawrence J. Walker, Brenda Lee, Amanda Riches, and William Dunlop. 2012. "Hierarchical Integration of Agency and Communion: A Study of Influential Moral Figures." *Journal of personality*, 80, 4, 1117-45. DOI: 10.1111/j.1467-6494.2012.00764.x.

Gill, Kate. August 14th 2022. "Climate activists fill golf course holes with cement to protest against water ban exemption." The Independent UK Edition Online.

Gilligan, Carol and John Michael Murphy. 1979. "Development from adolescence to adulthood: The philosopher and the dilemma of the fact." *New Directions for Child and Adolescent Development*, 85-99. https://doi.org/10.1002/cd.23219790507.

Glück, Judith, Bianca Gussnig, Sarah M. Schrottenbacher. 2019. "Wisdom and value orientations: Just a projection of our own beliefs?." *Journal of Personality*.1–23. https://doi.org/10.1111/ jopy.12530.

Glück, Judith and Robert J. Sternberg. 2022. "Wisdom, morality, and ethics." In *The Psychology of Wisdom: An Introduction*, edited by Robert J. Sternberg and Judith Glück, 118–134. Cambridge, UK: Cambridge University Press.

Greene, Joshua. 2013. *Moral tribes: Emotion, reason, and the gap between us and them.* New York: The Penguin Press.

Haan, Norma, Elaine Aerts, and Bruce A.B. Cooper. 1985. *On moral grounds: The search for practical morality.* New York: New York University Press.

Herman, Martyn. August 14, 2022. "Golf-French activists fill holes with cement in protest at watering exemptions." Reuters Online.

Kekes, John. 1983. "Wisdom." *American Philosophical Quarterly,* 20, 3, 277-286.

Parks, Rosa. November 2009. History Channel Online. www.history.com/topics/black-history/rosa-parks.

Robinson, Oliver. 2013. *Development through Adulthood: An Integrative Sourcebook.* Houndmills Basingstoke Hampshire: Palgrave Macmillan.

Schwartz, S. H. 2012. "An Overview of the Schwartz Theory of Basic Values." *Online Readings in Psychology and Culture*, 2, 1. https://doi.org/10.9707/2307-0919.1116.

Schwartz, Barry and Kenneth E. Sharpe. 2019. "Practical Wisdom: What Aristotle Might Add to Psychology." In *The Cambridge Handbook of Wisdom*, edited by Robert J. Sternberg and Judith Glück, 226–248. Cambridge, UK: Cambridge University Press.

Treviño, L.K., M. Brown, and L.P. Hartman. 2003. "A qualitative investigation of perceived executive ethical leadership: Perceptions from inside and outside the executive suite." *Human Relations*, 56, 1, 5-37.

Weststrate, Nic M., Michel Ferrari, and Monika Ardelt. 2016. "The many faces of wisdom: An investigation of cultural-historical wisdom exemplars reveals practical, philosophical, and benevolent prototypes." *Personality and Social Psychology Bulletin*, 42, 662–676. https://doi.org/10.1177/0146167216638075.

CHAPTER SIX

Achenbaum, W. Andrew and Lucinda Orwoll. 1991. "Becoming Wise: A Psycho-Gerontological Interpretation of the Book of Job." *The International Journal of Aging and Human Development*, 32, 1, 21-39. DOI:10.2190/419R-X8FC-Q6NE-0M85.

Colby, Anne and William Damon. 1992. *Some do care: Contemporary lives of moral commitment*. New York, NY: The Free Press.

Frankl, Viktor. E. 1984. *Man's search for meaning.* New York: Washington Square Press.

Glück, Judith and Robert J. Sternberg. 2022. "Wisdom, morality, and ethics." In *The Psychology of Wisdom: An Introduction*, edited by Robert J. Sternberg and Judith Glück, 118–134. Cambridge, UK: Cambridge University Press.

Story of Job:
https://www.britannica.com/topic/The-Book-of-Job.

Kesebir, Pelin. 2014. "A Quiet Ego Quiets Death Anxiety: Humility as an Existential Anxiety Buffer." *Journal of personality and social psychology*, 106, 610-23. 10.1037/a0035814.

Kramer, Deirdre. A. 2000. "Wisdom as a classical source of human strength: Conceptualization and empirical inquiry." *Journal of Social and Clinical Psychology,* 19, 1, 83–101.
https://doi.org/10.1521/jscp.2000.19.1.83.

Levenson, Michael, Patricia Jennings, Carolyn Aldwin, and Ray Shiraishi. 2005. "Self-Transcendence: Conceptualization and Measurement." *International journal of aging & human development,* 60, 127-43. 10.2190/XRXM-FYRA-7UoX-GRCo.

Malik, Kenan. May 24, 2020. "What the lessons from Auschwitz teach us about the choices we make." https://www.theguardian.com/commentisfree/2020/may/24/what-the-lessons-from-auschwitz-teach-us-about-the-choices-we-make.

Orwoll, Lucinda and Marion Perlmutter. 1990. "The Study of Wise Persons: Integrating a Personality Perspective." In *Wisdom: Its Nature, Origins, and Development,* edited by Robert J. Sternberg, 160–178. Cambridge, UK: Cambridge University Press.

Wayment, Heidi and Jack Bauer. 2017. "The quiet ego: concept, measurement, and well-being." In *The happy mind: Cognitive contributions to well-being,* edited by M. D. Robinson & M. Eid, 77–94. Switzerland: Springer International Publishing/Springer Nature. https://doi.org/10.1007/978-3-319-58763-9.

Wayment, Heidi A. and Jack J. Bauer. 2018. "The Quiet Ego: Motives for Self-Other Balance and Growth in Relation to Well-Being." *Journal of Happiness Studies*, 19, 881–896. https://doi.org/10.1007/s10902-017-9848-z.

Webster, Jeffrey Dean, Nic M. Weststrate, Michel Ferrari, Melanie Munroe, and Thomas W. Pierce. 2018. "Wisdom and Meaning in Emerging Adulthood." *Emerging Adulthood*, 6, 2, 118–136. https://doi.org/10.1177/2167696817707662.

Weststrate, Nic M. 2019. "The mirror of wisdom: self-reflection as a developmental precursor and core competency of wise people." In *The Cambridge Handbook of Wisdom*, edited by Robert J. Sternberg and Judith Glück, 500–518. Cambridge, UK: Cambridge University Press.

Weststrate, Nic M. and Judith Glück. 2017. "Hard-Earned Wisdom: Exploratory Processing of Difficult Life Experience is Positively Associated with Wisdom." *Developmental Psychology*, 53, 4, 800-814. 10.1037/dev0000286.

Worth, Piers and Matthew D. Smith. 2021. "Clearing the Pathways to Self-Transcendence." *Frontiers in Psychology*. April, 12:648381, pp.1-8. DOI: 10.3389/fpsyg.2021.648381.

Viktor Frankl Institute. n.d. Accessed April 3, 2023. https://www.viktorfrankl.org/.

Tangney, J. P. 2002. "Humility." In *Handbook of positive psychology*, edited by C. R. Snyder and S. J. Lopez, 411–419. Oxford, UK: Oxford University Press.

CHAPTER SEVEN

Ardelt, Monika. 2003. "Empirical Assessment of a Three-Dimensional Wisdom Scale." *Research on Aging*, 25, 275-324. 10.1177/0164027503025003004.

Ardelt, Monika. 2008. "Self-development through selflessness: The paradoxical process of growing wiser." In *Transcending self-interest: Psychological explorations of the quiet ego*, edited by Heidi Wayment and Jack Bauer, 221–233. Washing DC: American Psychological Association.

Glück, Judith. 2022. "The Development of Wisdom." In *The Psychology of Wisdom: An Introduction*, edited by Robert J. Sternberg and Judith Glück, 175–192. Cambridge, UK: Cambridge University Press.

Krafcik, Drew. 2015. "Words from the wise: Exploring the lives, qualities, and opinions of wisdom exemplars." *Integral Review: A Transdisciplinary & Transcultural Journal for New Thought, Research, & Praxis*, 11, 7–35. March.

Schwartz, Barry and Kenneth E. Sharpe. 2019. "Practical Wisdom: What Aristotle Might Add to Psychology." In *The Cambridge Handbook of Wisdom*, edited by Robert J. Sternberg and Judith Glück, 226–248. Cambridge, UK: Cambridge University Press.

Staudinger, Ursula and Ute Kunzmann. 2005. "Positive Adult Personality Development." *European Psychologist*, 10, 4, 320–329. 10.1027/1016-9040.10.4.320.

Walsh, Roger. 2015. "What is Wisdom? Cross-Cultural and Cross-Disciplinary Syntheses." *Review of General Psychology*, 19, 3, 278–293. https://doi.org/10.1037/gpr0000045.

Webster, Jeffrey Dean, Nic M. Weststrate, Michel Ferrari, Melanie Munroe, and Thomas W. Pierce. 2018. "Wisdom and Meaning in Emerging Adulthood." *Emerging Adulthood*, 6, 2, 118–136. https://doi.org/10.1177/2167696817707662.

Weststrate, Nic M. and Judith Glück. 2017. "Hard-earned wisdom: exploratory processing of difficult life experience is positively associated with wisdom." *Developmental Psychology*, 53, 800-814. 10.1037/dev0000286.

CHAPTER EIGHT

BBC News Article. September 8, 2022. "Queen Elizabeth II: Former prime ministers reflect on monarch's reign." Accessed April 17, 2023. https://www.bbc.co.uk/news/uk-politics-62844813.

Bates, Stephen. August 26, 2020. "Sir Ken Robinson obituary: Educationist who argued that children's creativity is stifled by school systems that prioritise academic achievement.' The Guardian Online. https://www.theguardian.com/education/2020/aug/26/sir-ken-robinson-obituary.

Bassett, Caroline L. 2011. "Wisdom and its development: Learning to become wise(r)." 2011. In *The Oxford Handbook of Reciprocal Adult Development and Learning* (2nd Ed.) edited by Carol Hoare, 302-317. Oxford, UK: Oxford University Press.

Colby, Anne and William Damon. 1992. *Some do care: Contemporary lives of moral commitment*. New York, NY: The Free Press.

Damon, William. 2004. "The Moral Advantage: how to succeed in business by doing the right thing. San Francisco, California: Berrett-Koehler Publishers, Inc.

De Pree, Max. 1989. "Leadership is an Art." New York: Bantam Doubleday Dell Publishing Group.

Gross, Daniel A. September 14, 2016. "How Should South Africa Remember the Architect of Apartheid?" Smithsonian Magazine, Accessed April 21, 2023 https://www.smithsonianmag.com/history/how-should-south-africa-remember-architect-apartheid-180960449/.

Hall, Stephen S. 2010. *Wisdom: From philosophy to neuroscience.* New York: Alfred A. Knopf.

Michigan State University. Overcoming Apartheid Building Democracy. https://overcomingapartheid.msu.edu/people. php?kid=163-574-649.

Kenneth Robinson "Do Schools Kill Creativity?" TED Talks, 2006, 19:12 minutes, https://www.ted.com/talks/sir_ken_robinson_do_ schools_kill_creativity/c.

Sir Ken Robinson's official website. https://www.sirkenrobinson.com.

Royal Central. Official website of the British Royal family. https://www.royal.uk/her-majesty-the-queen.

Sternberg, R.J., A. Reznitskaya, A., and L. Jarvin, L. July 2007. "Teaching for wisdom: what matters is not just what students know, but how they use it." *London Review of Education*, 5, 2, 143–158.

Zatz, Sydney. February 6, 2023. "71 years ago, Prince Philip conducted his saddest duty—telling his wife she was now Queen." Royal Central Online. https://royalcentral.co.uk/features/71-years-ago-prince-philip-conducted-his-saddest-duty-telling-his-wife-she-was-now-queen-186243/.

CONCLUSION

Bromley, Blake. 2014. "The Humor of Nelson Mandela." HuffPost Online. https://www.huffpost.com/entry/the-humor-of-nelson-mand_b_4402695.

Jeste, Dilip V. and Scott LaFee. 2020. *Wiser: The scientific roots of wisdom, compassion, and what makes us good.* Sounds True, Boulder, Colorado 80306.